1515 Capital of Texas
Highway S, Suite 107
Austin, TX 78746
512-329-8091 voice
512-329-6051 fax
ray@bardpress.com
www.bardpress.com

Dear Reader,

What a response! I anticipated a big success in 1998 when I discovered and published the original collection of the Wizard's letters to his clients, but what has happened since then has surprised even me. *The Wizard of Ads* was named Business Book of the Year and has sold thousands and thousands of copies. Roy H. Williams's (a.k.a. the Wizard) second book, in the fall of 1999, was a #1 *Wall Street Journal* and *New York Times* business bestseller and reached a far larger audience.

In this book I have been able to persuade the Wizard to share the secrets that he teaches at his renowned Academy. Over the last few years, people from the world's largest corporations, universities, publications, and advertising agencies have traveled to Buda, Texas, to spend a few days with the Wizard. From Procter and Gamble to the University of Michigan, from *USA Today* to J. Walter Thompson, CEOs, professors, columnists, and account executives have learned from the Wizard.

Roy H. Williams is a most amazing explorer. He is constantly looking for new truths. In this new book, he draws from a wide range of disciplines — chaos theory, neuroscience, art, literature, and poetry among them. As graduates of the Academy know, these principles can be applied in all areas of our business and personal lives.

I know you will enjoy and benefit from this latest edition of the Wizard's powerful secrets and magnetic storytelling.

Ray Bard
Publisher

PTOLEMY & WORLD MAPS

Nicolaus Germanus introduces trapezoidal (Donis) projection and adds modern maps to his Ptolemy ms, (Italy) 1466-82.

Ulm Ptolemy, M Germanus, woodcuts, 1482-86

Erhard and Waldseemüller's version of Glareanus of Central Europe, 1490?

Martellus Germanus, World drawing for Columbus discoveries

BEHAIM GLOBE, First detailed terrestrial globe based on Ptolemy

Etzlaub, map of Germany, showing roads, 1492 + 1501, etc.

Stabius-Werner projection

J. Ruysch, World 1508

WALDSEEMÜLLER, World map of Europe on STRASSBURG PTOLEMY 1513, 20 modern maps

Schöner, globes of 1515-20 showing Terra Australis

Peter APIANUS, Cosmographia 1524

Jacob of Deventer, Netherlands 1536-39

Gerardus MERCATOR, World 1538, 1512-94

Sebastian Münster, Cosmographia, 1544

Caspar Vopel, Cologne, Globes, etc

Mercator, Europe 1554

Diego Gutierrez, America, Antwerp 1562

Philip Apianus, Bavarische Landtafeln,

Mercator projection, World map 1569

A ORTELIUS, THEATRUM ORBIS TERRARUM 1570

Hogenberg-Höfnagel, Civitates Orbis Terrarum

Gerard de Jode, Speculum Orbis Terrarum

J Metelius, Itinerarium Orbis Christiani, 1579

WAGHENAER, Spieghel der Zeevaerdt

Plancius, World 1592

W Barentszoon, Mediter. Charts 1595

Mercator's Atlas, 1595

Hondius, typus orbis 1590

Henricus HONDIUS, Atlas of Mercator, World 1606-08 etc.

Bertius, Atlases

J A RAUCH, Quadrifidi Quadratorum

W Janssen BLAEU, Atlas Novus 1634-45

J JANSSOON, Nieuwe Atlas

Jan, Gerel. BLAEU, Atlas Major 1662-65

SEA ATLASES

Doncker, van Loon, P. Goos, All showing American charts

Van Keulen, 1681, etc.

De Hooge, 1695, etc.

De Wit, Atlas, 1675, 168, etc.

Homann house founded Nuremberg

Allard's Atlas, 1743

ENGLAND

Lily, England 1546

Lhuyd, England, 1569

Chr SAXTON, County maps

C Molyneux, Globes 1592

J Norden, Estate surveys

Edward WRIGHT, World in Mercator proj, 1600

Timothy Pont, Scotland

J Speed, Theatre of Great Britaine, 1610

Robt Dudley, Arcano del Mare, Florence 1646

Survey of Ireland, ms

Seller's Charts

Ogilby's Britannia

R Blome, "

Seller, Halley, Magnetic chart &

English Blaeu, 1689 etc.

Thornton, Philip Lea + others

Shalton's tapestry maps

Morden, Geography maps, 1700

OTHERS

Conrad Türst, Helvetia

Petri Rosselli, Chart of Atlantic

Nic. Claudianus, Bohemia 1518

B Wapowski, Poland

Ziegler, Scandinavia 1532

Tschudi, Helvetia 1538

OLAUS MAGNUS, Scand. 39

Anton Wied, Muscovy '44

Herberstein, Russia 49

Lazius, Austria + Hungary

Jenkinson, Russia 1562

J. le Moyne, Florida, 1563

Fabricius, Moravia 69

John White, Virginia manors

Oder, Saxonia 1585

A Bureus, Sweden

Strozarini (Spain) map, N America

Smith, Powell, Virginia 1612

CHAMPLAIN, St Lawrence 1613

Schikhart, Württemberg

W Wood, Massachusetts 1635

Baazplan, Ukraine 1648

J Mejer of Husum, Den.

M Martini, SJ, China atlas 55

I Voss, De Nili 79

Godunov, Russia + Siberia

A Hermann, Survey of Md + Va

Jesuit map of C Superior 72

S Joliet, Mississippi R.

Hennepin, North America

Remezov, Atlas of Siberia

It won't be long. You'll turn on your television or radio to find another company "branding" itself with an animal or quirky icon, but this time it won't stick. Critical mass: your mental motel with no vacancies, branding consultants going broke, businesses wondering what's wrong with their colorful logos and positioning statements.

Ideas and books on the rules of advertising work -- about as often as they fail. Explaining how, but not why, to advertise a particular way, step-and-method advertising is doomed. Such thinking neglects the reality that powerful persuasion is organic, changing. So, the Wizard requests, Don't ask me <u>what</u> works. Ask me <u>why</u> it works. What makes a thing persuasive? What makes it memorable? Unpredictable? Irresistible?

Ask, and the Wizard responds with principles -- principles found not in old TV reels or newspaper stacks, but in arts and sciences. He acquaints you with the poet and the painter, the photographer and the physicist. In dusty, cloth-covered volumes and glossy new science journals, he finds principles ignored or forgotten and helps you apply them to the art and science of life. But for all the practical ideas found in this book, for all the possible applications, the Wizard will tell you: Don't look for answers here. Look here for the right questions.

Chris J. Maddock
Wizard's First Assistant

OTHER BOOKS BY ROY H. WILLIAMS

The Wizard of Ads: Turning Words into Magic and Dreamers into Millionaires

Secret Formulas of the Wizard of Ads

Accidental Magic: The Wizard's Techniques for Writing Words Worth 1,000 Pictures

MAGICAL WORLDS

OF

the Wizard

of Ads

Roy H. Williams

BARD PRESS

AUSTIN
❖
ATLANTA

MAGICAL WORLDS OF
the Wizard of Ads

Bard Press
An imprint of Longstreet Press
2140 Newmarket Parkway, Suite 122
Marietta, GA 30067
770-980-1488 voice, 770-859-9894 fax
www.bardpress.com

Ordering Information
To order additional copies, contact your local bookstore or call 800-945-3132.
Quantity discounts are available.
ISBN 1-885167-52-0 trade paperback, 1-885167-53-9 hardcover

Library of Congress Cataloging-in-Publication Data

Williams, Roy H.
    Magical worlds of the wizard of ads : tools and techniques for
profitable persuasion / Roy H. Williams.
        p.   cm.
    Includes index.
    ISBN 1-885167-53-9 -- ISBN 1-885167-52-0 (pbk.)
    1. Advertising. I. Title.

    HF5823 .W495 2001
    659.1--dc21   2001037717

The author may be contacted at the following address:
Roy H. Williams
Williams Marketing, Inc.
1760 FM 967
Buda, TX 78610
512-295-5700 voice, 512-295-5701 fax
www.WizardofAds.com

Credits

Developmental Editor: Pennie Williams
Editor: Jeff Morris
Proofreaders: Deborah Costenbader, Luke Torn
Index: Linda Webster
Cover design: Hespenheide Design
Text design/production: Jeff Morris

First printing: August 2001

Contents

PART THE FIRST: ARCHITECTURE OF THE MIND

In Which the Wizard Examines the Question: "What Makes People Think the Way They Do?"

PART THE SECOND: TOOLS FOR PROFITABLE PERSUASION

In Which the Wizard Provides the Means of Using the Unique Capabilities of Your Mind to Best Effect

PART THE THIRD: CHARTING YOUR DESTINY & DREAMS

In Which the Wizard Shows You How to Light the Room without Burning the Candle at Both Ends

PART THE FOURTH: WIZARDS AT LARGE

In Which the Wizard Recounts Tales of Persons Exemplifying the Principles upon Which Wizardry Is Founded

Part the First

Architecture of the Mind

In Which the Wizard Examines the Question: "What Makes People Think the Way They Do?"

1
Speaking Worlds into Existence

In the book of Beginnings, an entire universe is spoken into existence with the words, "Let there be light." Badda-bing, badda-boom, the Big Bang. As soon as the lights are on, the Creator continues by saying, "Let there be this," and "Let there be that," until everything has been spoken into existence except you and me. Finally, near the end of chapter one, He says, "Let us make man in our own image. . . ."

Wait a minute. If, in fact, God said, "I'm going to make some little miniatures of myself," and if, in fact, two of these little miniatures are you and I, then why can't WE speak worlds into existence?

Oh, but we can. You and I speak worlds into existence every day. Each time we describe an experience or tell a story, we speak that world into existence in the minds of those around us.

A gleam of light came straight through the opening into the bay and fell on the smooth rock-face. There was a loud crack. A flake of rock split from the wall and fell. A hole appeared suddenly about three feet from the ground.

Quickly, trembling lest the chance should fade, the dwarves rushed to the rock and pushed — in vain.

"The key! The key!" cried Bilbo. "Where is Thorin?"

Thorin hurried up.

"The key!" shouted Bilbo. "The key that went with the map! Try it now while there is still time!"

Then Thorin stepped up and drew the key on its chain from round his neck. He put it to the hole. It fitted and it turned! Snap! The gleam went out, the sun sank, the moon was gone, and evening sprang into the sky.

Now they all pushed together, and slowly a part of the rock-wall gave way. Long straight cracks appeared and widened. A door five feet high and three feet wide was outlined, and slowly without a sound swung inwards. It seemed as if darkness flowed out like a vapor from the hole in the mountain-side, and deep darkness in which nothing could be seen lay before their eyes, a yawning mouth leading in and down.

Bilbo and Thorin were spoken into existence by J. R. R. Tolkien in his book *The Hobbit*. Are you beginning to understand the awesome force that hides behind your lips? You speak a new world into existence every time you utter a few simple words of encouragement. Words of romance create new worlds every day. And how often have words of persuasion created a brave new world!

New worlds are only a few words away. Would you like to learn to harness this amazing energy?

Hang on, it's going to be a wild ride.

A powerful agent is the right word. Whenever we come upon one of those intensely right words in a book or a newspaper, the resulting effect is physical as well as spiritual, and electrically prompt.

Mark Twain

2

Perceptual Realities

oet John Godfrey Saxe (1816–1887) tells of six men of Indostan, "to learning much inclined, who went to see the Elephant (though all of them were blind), that each by observation might satisfy his mind."

Those who have read Saxe's poem will recall that the first blind man felt the broad side of the animal and proclaimed the elephant "to be very like a wall." The second, feeling the elephant's tusk, was startled: "Did you say wall? But an elephant is like a spear!" Wrestling with the elephant's squirming trunk, the third said, "Wall? Spear? The elephant is like a snake!" The fourth man, feeling the elephant's knee, said, "Idiots! The elephant is like a tree!" The fifth, feeling the ear, said, "Have you all gone crazy? An elephant is like a fan!" The sixth man, feeling the tail, said, "Any fool can see that an elephant is like a rope."

In perceptual reality, each of the men was correct.

I tell this story because most efforts at human persuasion are little more than one blind man urging another blind man to "see" the elephant as he does.

Have you ever paused to consider that your family, your friends, your co-workers, and your customers live in their own private, perceptual realities? Instead of expecting them all to see the elephant as you do, why not try to see what they're seeing? If you're patient, you will finally see enough of the elephant from different perspectives to finally make sense of it all.

And then you'll have something to say that will really be worth hearing.

Many of the truths we cling to
depend greatly on our point of view.

Obi-Wan Kenobi

3

Time and Perceptual Reality

All movement happens in space — height, width, and depth, the first three dimensions. The fourth dimension is time.

Light moves through space, and according to Einstein, time stands still at the speed of light. Light is the pendulum of the universe, marking and measuring time.

And just as faith is the evidence of things not seen, color is the evidence of light. Color is the momentary, visible bridge between space and time.

Time is also the mirror in which our choices are seen. And it is through our choices that our values and beliefs are revealed. If you want to know what a person believes, you need only to watch what he does.

Question: If objective, four-dimensional reality is this meeting place we call the space-time continuum (composed of height, width, depth, and time), then what is three-dimensional reality?

Answer: A reality outside of time.

Height, width, and depth are the realm of the dorsolateral prefrontal association area of the brain — imagination, where personal, three-dimensional realities live and thrive amidst your brain's ten thousand billion synapses. Most of your life will take place in three-dimensional reality.

The fourth dimension, time, is simply where your three-dimensional realities overlap with mine.

The objective of human persuasion is to introduce a three-dimensional reality into the mind of others, causing them to imagine doing what you want them to do. Once this is accomplished, the step from the three-dimensional reality of their minds into this meeting place called the fourth dimension is a very short step indeed.

See ch. 10, "Waxing Woo-Woo," ch. 11, "Dimensional Realities 2, 3, & 4," and ch. 19, "The Tollbooth on the Yellow Brick Road."

Question: Are three-dimensional realities really real?

Answer: They are as real as a mother's love. Although the love of a mother does not exist in physical, objective reality, there are few who would say that it is not real. A mother's love is perceptual reality, three-dimensional reality, a reality outside of time.

Are there truly realities outside of time? Certainly! It was to one such three-dimensional, perceptual reality — freedom — that the signers of our Declaration of Independence pledged their lives, their fortunes, and their sacred honor.

Advertising cannot change objective, four-dimensional reality, but it can powerfully change perceptual, three-dimensional reality. Your customer's expectations are three-dimensional, perceptual realities. The right words can modify, change, and adjust these. To what degree do you need to modify the public's awareness of you? How much do you need to adjust what they may or may not have heard about you, your product, or your company? ᴄᴂ

"The time of physics is defined and measured by a pendulum, whether it is the pendulum of a grandfather's clock, the pendulum of the Earth's rotation around the sun, or the pendulum of the precessing electron in the nuclear magnetic field of the hydrogen maser. Time, therefore, is defined by periodic rotation — that is, by motion related to a point moving uniformly around a circle."

— Physicist
Edgar Lipworth,
as reported by the
occasionally apocryphal
but always colorful
Tom Robbins

4

Will You Ever Face Reality?

> Nothing exists except atoms and empty space; everything else is opinion.
>
> — Democritus

Whether you're a manager trying to motivate a staff member, a parent trying to win the cooperation of a child, a sales professional trying to convince a customer, or an ad writer trying to grow a business, your goal is to persuade someone else to see things "your way."

Human persuasion is nothing more than the successful introduction and guided progression of a series of mental images, artfully presented to create a compelling perceptual reality — that is, a three-dimensional reality, one that exists outside of time, the fourth dimension. If this concept seems a little abstract, just think of perceptual realities as "imaginings."

Central to every effort in human persuasion is the fact that people can do only those things they have first imagined. Your job is to get them to imagine doing what you want them to do. "I don't go for all that foo-foo stuff!" bellows the skeptic. "I just believe in giving people the pure, objective facts. I believe in sticking to reality."

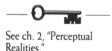

See ch. 2, "Perceptual Realities."

Q: Is it possible to communicate pure, objective reality? Or even to experience it? For the answer, we turn to the brilliant Brazilian neurologist Dr. Jorge Martins de Oliveira.

A: "Our perception does not identify the outside world as it really is, but the way that we are allowed to recognize it, as a consequence of transformations performed by our senses. We experience electromagnetic waves, not as waves, but as images and colors. We experience vibrating objects, not as vibrations, but as sounds. We experience chemical compounds dissolved in air or water, not as chemicals, but as specific smells and tastes. Colors, sounds, smells, and tastes are products of our minds, built from sensory experiences. They do not exist, as such, outside our brain. Actually, the universe is colorless, odorless, insipid, and silent."*

Q: Hmm. . . . Okay, doctor. But might there not be "objective sensory facts"?

A: "Although you and I share the same biological architecture and function, perhaps what I perceive as a distinct color and smell is not exactly equal to the color and smell you perceive. We may give the same name to similar perceptions, but we cannot know how they relate to the reality of the outside world. Perhaps we never will."

So if according to modern neurology, even our most objective and detailed first-person exposures are altered and colored by the perspective that we bring to an experience, what makes us think we can communicate "objectively" to the second person?

The first step in honest communication is to abandon the myth of an objective perspective. Those who claim they can offer it are either hopelessly naïve or dazzlingly arrogant.

Never hesitate to describe with confidence your own feelings, perceptions, and opinions. In the world of perceptual reality, there is no one with higher authority than you. ᏻ

* "Therefore, we can now safely answer one of the eternal questions of traditional philosophy: Does a sound exist when a tree falls in a forest, if no one is there to hear it? The answer must obviously be, 'No. The fall of the tree creates vibrations. Sound occurs only if those vibrations are perceived by a living thing.'"

— Dr. Jorge Martins de Oliveira

5

Reality Begins with Imagination

by Robin Frederick

I am a big proponent of fantasies. After all, everything in life starts with an idea — from a Fortune 500 company to a great painting to a romantic fantasy. Ideas become reality when we put energy into them, especially emotional energy. Studies have shown that the emotion accompanying an idea or image causes it to realize itself — the more emotion, the more quickly the idea becomes reality. By using music to evoke emotions, you give your fantasy a passionate, single-minded energy that can propel it right into your life. Or, as Billy Ocean once put it, ". . . outta my dreams and into my car."

Like some mythological beast — half speech, half music — songs have a seemingly magical power to revive long-forgotten memories and give voice to our deepest feelings. In fact, songs speak directly to some of the most primitive parts of the brain, evoking deeply felt emotional responses, triggering involuntary recall of events, and conveying powerful messages while essentially bypassing the rational, analytical areas of the mind.

The Inner Critic is that little voice that believes you do not deserve abundant love, good health, or success. But this is only the opinion of one part of your brain — your judgmental, analytical, rational left brain. There is a whole area of your brain that doesn't make judgments at all, and it is here that songs are processed and make their deepest impression.

Although the ability to speak and form thoughts into words and sentences rests almost exclusively with the left side of the brain, understanding the emotional tone of voice is a function of the right side. Thus both sides of the brain are needed to correctly interpret

With over 500 songs produced for television and record albums, Robin Frederick is regarded as one of the premier music producers in the field of family entertainment. Her work with such characters as Bugs Bunny, Mickey Mouse, Winnie the Pooh, and the Little Mermaid has delighted children for well over a decade.

the content of spoken words, with most of that activity taking place on the left side. But when these same words are sung, the left/right division of labor shifts dramatically. Lyrics are absorbed and processed almost exclusively in the "nonverbal" right hemisphere. In fact, neurologists have reported that when the left hemisphere of the brain is sedated (or damaged), the subject is unable to speak but can still sing words. If the right hemisphere is impaired, the person can speak normally but cannot sing (Anthony Storr, *Music and the Mind*). In songs, then, the right hemisphere is handling the verbal information rather than the normally dominant left hemisphere.

Now, there's a funny thing about the right side of your brain — it is not concerned with making judgments or assessing the factual truth of a statement; that's the left brain's job. And there's yet another way in which words can sneak their message past your Inner Critic. . . . Good poets make extensive use of "right-brain language." Forget that sensible, linear, factual, left-brain speech. The language of the right brain is a horse of a different color. A riot of imagery, a cascade of connections, sensations, and associations. The right brain speaks in metaphors, juxtapositions, and similes, using a whole range of poetic devices to express the inexpressible and describe the indescribable. Emotions? No problem. Hearts soar. Lips taste like wine. Eyes are mirrors of the soul. Imagine what your left brain thinks of that. Utter nonsense! Not worth even bothering about! But to your illogical, intuitive right brain, it's perfectly clear.

Reprinted by permission from Robin Frederick's web page, www.soundexp.com.

It is through science that we prove,
but through intuition that we discover.

Henri Poincaré

6

Left, Right, Left, Right, Left, Right

Your brain is divided into two main sections, or hemispheres. The left brain is logical, linear, and objective, and focuses on details. The right brain is intuitive, chaotic, and subjective, and sees the "big picture." The hemisphere you prefer to use in responding to sensory input determines much of your personality and behavior. If you react to life using your left-hemisphere abilities (analysis and logic), you are "left-brain dominant." If you usually favor your right hemisphere (emotion and intuition), you're "right-brain dominant." These choices don't mean that the other half of your brain is impaired in any way — merely that you prefer one hemisphere over the other. An ability to "switch" hemispheres (to call upon the appropriate hemisphere at the appropriate moment) is the mark of a balanced and well-adjusted individual.*

Chaos is not randomness.

* Summary of Left/Right Brain, by On Purpose Associates (www.Funderstanding.com)

In our schools, left-brain scholastic subjects focus on logical thinking, analysis, and accuracy; right-brain subjects emphasize aesthetics, feeling, and creativity. In America, not just our educational system but our very culture favors left-brain styles of thinking and downplays right-brain ones. Where did we get this strong bias toward the logical left half of the brain? Amazingly, it came to us as standard equipment when we adopted the English language.

See ch. 24, "Did Your Valedictorian Get Rich?"

Addressing his Japanese countrymen, MIT professor Susumu Tonegawa, winner of the 1987 Nobel Prize in Medicine, said, "We should consider changing our thinking process in the field of science by trying to reason in English." Dr. Tonegawa wasn't saying that English is better than Japanese — only that English is better than Japanese for purposes of scientific research, which is a way of saying that English has a particular ideological basis that Japanese does not. We call that ideological basis the "scientific outlook." (If the scientific outlook seems natural to you, as it does to me, it is because our language makes it so.) What we think of as "reasoning" is determined by the character of our language. To reason in Japanese is not the same thing as to reason in English or Italian or German.

To put it simply, language has an ideological agenda that is likely to be hidden from view. That agenda is so deeply integrated with our personalities and worldview that a special effort is required to detect its presence. Language appears to us to be only a natural extension of who and what we are. This is the great secret of language: Because it comes from inside us, we incorrectly believe it to be a direct, unedited, unbiased expression of how the world really is.**

** Tonegawa story from *Technopoly*, by Neil Postman

As an example of the strong bias of the English language, let's examine the common use of the directions "up" and "down" as metaphors that imply good and bad.

• **Conscious is up; unconscious is down:** Wake *up*. I'm *up* already. I'm an early *riser*. I *dropped* off and *fell* asleep. The patient *went under* anesthesia, *sank* into a coma, then *dropped* dead.

• **Controlling is up; being controlled is down:** He's *on top* of the situation, in *high* command, at the *height* of power in having so many people *under* him. His influence started to *decline*, until he *fell* from power and *landed* as *low man* on the totem pole, back at the *bottom* of the heap.

• **Good is up; bad is down:** *High*-quality work made this a *peak* year and put us *over the top*. Things were looking *up* when the market *bottomed out* and hit an all-time *low*. It's been *downhill* ever since.

• **Rational (left brain) is up; emotional (right brain) is down:** I *pulled myself up* from this sorry state and had a *high-level* intellectual discussion with my therapist, a *high-minded, lofty* individual. My heart *sank* and I was in the *depth* of despair, unable to *rise* above my emotions.***

*** "Up" and "down" examples taken from *The Man Who Tasted Shapes*, by Richard Cytowic, M.D.

Yes, as odd as this may sound, America's strong bias in favor of left-brain logic (and against emotion) was dictated when we adopted English as our native tongue. Is it beginning to make more sense to you why French, Italian, Spanish, Latin, and Portuguese are called the "Romantic" (right-brain) languages? ❧

7

Music, Math, and the Mind

Employing magnetic resonance imaging to peek into the inner workings of the human brain, Harvard Medical School recently published a study indicating that certain parts of the brains of musicians grow 7 percent larger on average than their nonmusical peers'.

In a simultaneous but unrelated study, researchers from the University of California found that second-graders who took piano lessons averaged 27 percent higher scores on math skills than their nonmusical friends. Students who were given the most intensive type of music training (the Kodaly method) scored highest of all.

Prior to these announcements, the fact that Mozart often scribbled algebraic equations alongside his musical compositions was considered irrelevant historical trivia.

Mind-boggling, isn't it?

I was listening to Dan Davis one Sunday morning when — click! — the whole thing suddenly made sense. Dan was in the middle of making a much larger point when he casually mentioned that "math is a language like English or French or Chinese, except that it's much more precise. In the language of math, relationships are expressed with precision and certainty. Math is a language that allows us to communicate concepts that could not possibly be expressed in any other way."

Spanish and Greek are by no means the same language, but they are in the same family of languages. Due to similar verb conjugation structures, speakers of Greek have an advantage over speakers of English when it comes to learning Spanish.

You've already figured it out, right? Music is a language in the same family as math. When proficiency in one is extended, ability in the other is expanded as well. This little nugget of insight sent me in search of other pairs of talents that might be connected in the mind. Digging and probing through the blueprints of human persuasion, I found some things I think will interest you.

Today the treacherous, unexplored areas of the world are not in continents or the seas; they are in the minds and hearts of men.

Allen E. Claxton, D.D.

8

Dual Movie Screens

I would rather live in a world where my life is surrounded by mystery than live in a world so small that my mind could comprehend it.

— Harry Emerson Fosdick

Each hemisphere of your brain contains a mental movie screen. In your right brain, that screen provides an awesome, 360-degree global vista that extends above, below, and all around you. Watching this mental movie screen is like floating weightlessly in the middle of a vast, translucent bubble with a million glowing scenes bouncing off its inner walls. Warm, dazzling colors reach out to you from each image. Twisting and turning in every direction, you see amazing new things from each new perspective. Unfortunately, your right brain is nonverbal, so you must find the words to express all this within the tight confines of your brain's left half.

The sad little movie screen of your left brain is much too small to reveal anything grand. It shows only flat (two-dimensional), black-and-white images. As if that weren't bad enough, a legalistic little theater manager insists that every complex concept be broken down into its component pieces so that they can be examined separately on the left brain's little black-and-white screen.

See ch. 5, "Reality Begins with Imagination."

When your rational left brain is confronted with something that is too big to comprehend, it simply compresses, reduces, and dismantles the thing until it is small enough to fit neatly onto the little screen. The left brain compresses complex data until it begins to tell us things that are not true. It compresses complexities within music until we no longer hear all that is there. The left brain will not rest until it has figured out a way to make everything in life fit within the realm of the "completely knowable." Consequently, that which is complex and wonderful is often compressed until there is nothing left but a bloodless shadow of the original wonder.

Tragically, this left-brain view of the world is regarded as the scientific perspective, and the miniaturized, black-and-white images revealed on the left brain's movie screen are the ones considered to be factual. But thank heavens, not every scientist worships at the left brain's bureaucratic altar:

> I maintain that the human mystery is incredibly demeaned by reductionism, with its claim in promissory materialism to account eventually for all of the spiritual world in terms of patterns of neural activity. This belief must be classed as a superstition. We are spiritual beings with souls in a spiritual world, as well as material beings with bodies and brains existing in a material world.
>
> — John Eccles, Nobel Prize–winning neurologist

Can ideas be communicated in such a way that massive, right-brain images can be seen on the little left-brain screen? Certainly. The secret is to use symbolic thought. In her book *Powers of Ten*, Phyllis Morrison uses luscious symbolic language in speaking of one of the wonders of physics: "It reaches inside every candy box, no matter what the wrapping, to distinguish the full pound from the empty container." (What a cool way to describe gravity! You go, Phyllis!)

You haven't been thinking with only half a mind, have you?

My father says that almost the whole world is asleep. Everybody you know, everybody you see, everybody you talk to. He says that only a few people are awake and they live in a state of constant, total amazement.

Meg Ryan to Tom Hanks in *Joe vs. the Volcano*

9

Invisible, But Real Nonetheless

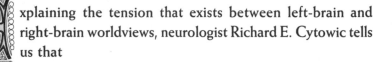

Explaining the tension that exists between left-brain and right-brain worldviews, neurologist Richard E. Cytowic tells us that

Plato said that we are prisoners of our feelings and that we should therefore hold fast to the sacred cord of reason [left brain] lest we be lost. Aristotle, on the other hand, argued with Plato that emotions have a logic of their own [right-brain intuition] and must be understood on their own terms. The American public, however, is more inclined to favor Plato's dichotomy that emotions conflict with, and threaten reason.

Speaking of his own experience, Dr. Cytowic says,

My innate analytic personality had been reinforced by twenty years of training in science and medicine. I reflexively analyzed whatever passed my way and firmly believed that the intellect could conquer everything through reason. I had never considered that there might be more to the human mind than the rational part that I was familiar with. It had never once occurred to me that a force to balance rationality existed, let alone that it might be a normal part of the human psyche. . . . Neuroscientists have just lately come to realize how important emotion is. Placing reason and the [intellectual] cortex first and foremost is like the Wizard of Oz shouting, "Pay no attention to the man behind the curtain." Reason and an accomplice called self-awareness have deluded us into believing that they have been pulling the strings, but emotion and mentation not normally accessible to self-awareness have been in charge all along.

Professor Neil Postman, communications theorist and winner of the George Orwell Award for Clarity in Language, makes a similar point:

In the Middle Ages, people believed in the authority of their religion, no matter what. Today, we believe in the authority of our science, no matter what. If I informed you that the paper on which this book is printed was made by a special process which uses the skin of a pickled herring, on what grounds would you dispute me? For all you know — indeed, for all I know — the skin of a pickled herring could have made this paper. And if the facts were confirmed by an industrial scientist who described to us some incomprehensible process by which it was done (employing, of course, encomial dyoxin,) we might both believe it. Or not wholly disbelieve it, since the ways of technology, like the ways of God, are awesome and mysterious.

P.S. Just for the record, there is no such thing as encomial dyoxin.

Whether it's science, technology, personal experience, true love, astrology, or gut feelings, each of us has confidence in something that we will never fully comprehend.

It's important that you understand that. ᥱᨺᥱ

Minds are like parachutes — they only function when open.

Thomas Dewar

10

Waxing Woo-Woo
by Chris Maddock

The opposite of a correct statement is a false statement. The opposite of a profound truth may well be another profound truth.

— Niels Bohr

Light is a wave. Experiments by Italian Jesuits confirmed this fact as early as 1681. Physics students in colleges around the world today still perform rudimentary experiments that prove light's wave nature.

But light is also a particle. It is made up of measurable quanta, or packets of energy, called photons. Light's particle nature can be tested and confirmed just as surely as its wave nature.

But it can't be both a wave and a particle, since waves and particles are, by definition, mutually exclusive. (A wave is something that moves on or through a substance at many points at one time. A particle, however, doesn't have to move through anything, and is measurable at only one place at one time.) Despite the fact that waves and particles are mutually exclusive, light can be observed as both a wave and a particle, depending on how you look at it.

Likewise, two of the twentieth century's most important scientific theories, general relativity and quantum mechanics, are mutually exclusive. But they are nonetheless separately true, and each is eminently verifiable.

General relativity, which provides such bizarre outcomes as speed-dependent aging and atomic bombs, has been proven and is successfully used every day. But the theory breaks down at the submicroscopic scales of quantum physics because it can't account for the noodle-bending reality that we can never know both the speed

Chris Maddock is First Assistant to the Wizard.

and the position of an object with certainty. Although both general relativity and quantum mechanics are demonstrably true, they are also mutually exclusive.

How can this be? How can our world contain mutually exclusive truths?

I don't know, and you don't either. The important fact is that it can and it does. What this means to you and me is that our definition for "truth" is far too small, our minds too linear, to grasp the greatest truths.

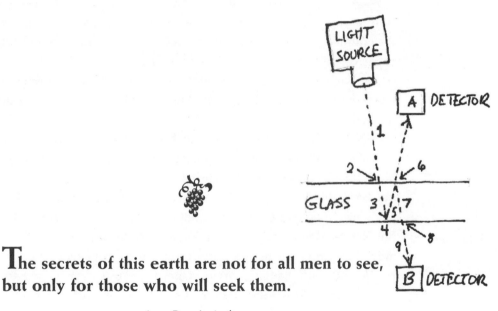

The secrets of this earth are not for all men to see, but only for those who will seek them.

Ayn Rand, *Anthem*

11

Dimensional Realities 2, 3, & 4

wo is the duality number. It speaks of separation, opposites, and conflict. Good/bad. Black/white. Up/down. Positive/negative. Right/wrong.

A rule is an example of two-dimensional thinking. With a rule, there are only two possibilities: right and wrong. Two-dimensional thinking can be illustrated by two points on a sheet of paper connected by a line. What do you see? A stick. Rules are like sticks. You can threaten, prod, and even beat people with them, but when the rule doesn't fit the situation, the only thing you can do is break it.

Three is the energy number. It speaks of activation, dynamism, and life. A world of color emerges from red, yellow, and blue. A world of matter springs from protons, neutrons, and electrons. A world of chaotic systems is launched by first, second, and third gravitating bodies.

Three-dimensional thinking is not linear. It isn't composed of rules, but is birthed in principles. A principle is like a rope in that it can be moved in three dimensions. Like a rope, principles readily conform to the shape of changing circumstances without ever having to be compromised. And principles are like ropes in one other way — you can lead people with them.

Four is the structure number. It speaks of stability, substance, and completion. Four seasons complete a year, four points complete a compass, and four legs stabilize a chair. When the fourth dimension (time) joins the first three dimensions (height, width, and depth), you have stable, objective reality. Four is structure.

Any problem involving human choice is a three-dimensional problem. Try to solve a three-dimensional problem with a series of

"Two is the separation of one thing from another and thus represents a state of conflict. Two implies opposition."

— Edward F. Edinger,
Ego and Archetype

"The number three is specifically associated with the creative process."

— H. G. Baynes,
Mythology of the Soul

two-dimensional rules and the invariable result will be the creation of a bureaucracy. The current IRS tax code is a classic example. Now at 2.8 million words and growing, it fills a stack of paper more than two feet thick. 🙠

See ch. 3, "Time and Perceptual Reality."

12

One Is the Only-est Number

Edinger speaks of one as "the number of unity." Or as Plotinus put it, "There must be something that is fully self-sufficient. That is, the one; it alone, within and without, is without need." In his *Parmenides* dialogue, Plato includes a lengthy discourse on the nature of one, saying, "The one is neither at rest nor in motion. . . . [T]he one has nothing to do with time and does not occupy any stretch of time. . . . [T]he one both is and is becoming older and younger than itself." According to Dr. Edinger, "The chief thing that Plato demonstrates is that the One cannot be apprehended by logic or the conscious categories of time, space, and causality. It cannot be apprehended by [left-brain] logic because it involves contradictions."

Evidently, the One is composed of mutually exclusive truths.

So if two is the number of opposition, and "right/wrong" rules are two-dimensional, left-brain realities . . . and if three is the number of possibilities, and principles and imaginings are three-dimensional, "perceptual" right-brain realities . . . and if four is the structure number and four-dimensional space-time is "literal" reality . . . is the colorless, odorless, insipid, and silent universe described by Dr. Jorge Martins de Oliveira in chapter 4 the only pure and objective first-dimensional reality: the reality of One?

If one-dimensional reality doesn't already have your head spinning, consider this: according to physicist Julian Barbour, the mutual exclusivity that exists between quantum mechanics and general relativity could easily be reconciled if time did not exist. Barbour states,

> The basic idea of my theory is that there isn't time as such. There is no invisible river of time that's flowing. But there are things that I would say that you could call an instant of time; or better, a now.

See ch. 3, "Time and Perceptual Reality," ch. 4, "Will You Ever Face Reality?", and ch. 11, "Dimensional Realities 2, 3, & 4."

As we live we seem to move through a succession of instants of time, nows, and the question is, what are they? They are where everything in the universe is at this moment, now.

Is it really possible that our sense of the passage of time is nothing more than a cosmic illusion? A lot of great minds are already embracing the notion. In *Black Holes and Baby Universes*, Stephen Hawking states, "I think that imaginary time will come to seem as natural as a round earth does now."

If quantum mechanics and general relativity were both here before time was created, then time is effectively a newcomer of relatively little consequence to them. In his book *A Brief History of Time*, Stephen Hawking says,

See ch. 10, "Waxing Woo-Woo."

This was first pointed out by St. Augustine. When he was asked, 'What did God do before he created the universe?' Augustine didn't reply. Instead, he said that time was a property of the universe that God created, and that time did not exist before the beginning of the universe.

Now I'm going to lie down and put a cold rag on my head. ⤶

**That's the problem with eternity —
there's no telling when it will end.**

Tom Stoppard

13

Four Kinds of Thought, Three Kinds of People

According to Dr. Ricardo Gattass of the Institute of Biophysics, all human thought can be classified as verbal, abstract, analytical, or symbolic.

1. In verbal thought, we experience a thought as if listening to our own voice. Using auditory memory, we translate ideas into words. Verbal thought is a left-brain process.

2. In analytical thought, we examine possibilities in a logical sequence relative to the goal of foreseeing. The objective of analytical thought is to forecast a result. Obviously, analytical thought is left brain.

3. Abstract thought is right brain and is utterly free. In abstract thought, intuition and emotion replace logic as we examine ideas and sensory experiences. The mental images created in abstract thought are unbounded by the physical world and often represent imaginary events.*

4. In symbolic thought, we consider a thing from different perspectives and then assess from each point the perspective of that angle of view. Musical understanding is symbolic thought. Similes and metaphors are symbolic thought as well, as we use symbolic thought to encode and decode associative memories. Symbolic thought bridges intuition and intellect, right brain and left. Symbolic thought is the key that opens both heart and mind.

The greatest teacher who ever lived used symbolic thought in 100 percent of his presentations. His use of simile and metaphor was legendary. He was forever saying things like "The kingdom of heaven [a right-brain, abstract concept] is like a mustard seed [a left-brain, factual concept]." He would then go on to explain how the two were alike.

* Remember, the human body contains nearly 100 million sensory receptors, allowing us to see, hear, taste, touch, and smell physical reality. But the brain contains more than 10,000 billion synapses. In other words, you and I are approximately 100,000 times better equipped to experience a world that does not exist than a world that does. Keep in mind that your prospects can do nothing they have not first seen themselves do in their minds. The goal of human persuasion is to cause others to imagine doing what you want them to do.

I was instantly reminded of these four kinds of thinking when I stumbled upon the following in *Principles of Philosophy, Volume I* by René Descartes:

> If we endeavor to form our conceptions upon history and life, we remark three classes of men. The first consists of those for whom the chief thing is the qualities of feelings. These men create art. The second consists of the practical men who carry on the business of the world. They respect nothing but power and respect power only so far as it is exercised. The third class consists of men to whom nothing seems great but reason. If force interests them, it is not in its exertion, but in that it has a reason and a law. For men of the first class, Nature is a picture; for men of the second class, it is an opportunity; for men of the third class it is a cosmos so admirable that to penetrate its ways seems to them the only thing that makes life worth living. These are the men whom we see possessed by a passion to teach and to disseminate their influences. If they do not give themselves over completely to their passions to learn, it is because they exercise self-control. These are natural scientific men, and they are the only men that have any real success in scientific research.

Did you see the connection between the quote and Dr. Gattass's four kinds of thought? Here's what I'm thinking: We all share a dependence on verbal thought, as it is verbal thought that allows us to communicate with one another. It is therefore our preferences among the remaining three types of thought that divide humanity into the three broad categories described by Descartes.

The first class (artists) prefer abstract thought, since their desire is to examine feelings. The second class (businesspeople) prefer analytical thought, because their principal objective is to forecast results. The third class (scientists) prefer symbolic thought, since their goal is to map and understand the interconnectedness of the cosmos.

Hmmm. . . . Arts. Business. Science. Aren't these the major divisions of curriculum in most colleges? ꙮ

The perfect management team contains a member from each of the three classes

14

Carolina on My Mind

The original release of this 1970 hit song by James Taylor had the title misspelled on both sides of the 45 rpm single. The song title was not "Carolina *on* My Mind," as the label clearly stated, but "Carolina *in* My Mind."

What's the difference?

Everything.

To have something "on" your mind is to consider it intellectually, to judge its relative merits based on all the data you've been able to acquire.

To go somewhere "in" your mind is to abandon left-brain analytical thought and to begin exploring the perceptual realities offered by right-brain abstract thought.

> In my mind, I'm goin' to Carolina
> Can't you see the sunshine?
> Can't you just feel the moonshine?
> Ain't he just like a friend of mine
> To hit me from behind?
> Yes, I'm goin' to Carolina in my mind
> Karen sees a silver sun
> You'd best walk her away and watch it shining
> Watch her watch the mornin' come. . . .

One of the great lyricists and musicians of our generation, James Taylor obviously knows how to create a perceptual reality, a reality outside of time. Through his eyes, you see sunshine, feel moonshine, and watch a girl named Karen as she watches the dawn.

In *The Wizard of Ads,* I said: "Emotion and intellect are two sides of a single coin. Win the heart and the mind will follow. People can go only to those places that they have already been in their minds. The secret of human persuasion is to cause people to imagine doing what you want them to do."

Most advertising is tedious because it is hacked from a concrete world of fact. Left brain speaks unto left brain, but right brain calls unto right.

If you prefer to "keep your feet on the ground" and "stick with the facts," go right ahead.

But I'm going to Carolina with James.

The difference between the right word and almost the right word is the difference between lightning and a lightning bug.

Mark Twain

15

The Duality Principle

From: "Kathleen & Wolfgang" <kathleenh@sympatico.ca>
To: <roy@wizardofads.com>
Subject: Thank you and here's a question
Date: Wed, Jan 31, 2001, 9:32 PM

Roy,

Your team is outstanding. Mark and I are blown away
with your real deal. Thank you for the wisdom and
understanding. It truly was the wisest investment
I've ever made in education. I miss you guys! I need
more. You are the cocaine of understanding.

Question for you. What is the duality principle?

Second question. Is business topology the APE
formulae as outlined in your second book or am I
missing something? p.s. I had to attempt to explain
third gravitating bodies to my best friend, and
wife. You won't believe it but she got it. I swear.
My GSM wants me to do a review with the staff. Do
you mind if I try the stuff on them?

Did I say I miss you kids? I really wish we could
have stayed for 1 more day.

Cheers,

Wolfgang Klein
Wizard Academy class of January, 2001

From: "Roy H. Williams" <Roy@WizardofAds.com>
To: "Kathleen & Wolfgang" <kathleenh@sympatico.ca>
Subject: Re: Thank you and here's a question
Date: Thu, Feb 1, 2001, 7:23 AM

Wolfgang,

You have a very smart wife. You're going to realize
just how smart she really is when you try to explain
3-D realities and 3rd gravitating bodies to your co-
workers and hear them say, "So what you're telling
me is that you just have to get three things
happening at once, right?" Very few people can grasp
the ideas of divergence and convergence within
patterns too big for the human mind. Compression
keeps most people from seeing 3rd gravitating bodies
when you try to explain the concept without first
having had the opportunity to stretch their minds a
little. (Perhaps a few years of being married to you
has provided all the mind-stretching that Kathleen
required to see and hear a world of 3rd gravitating
bodies all around her. . . .)

Go ahead and try to explain it to some other people.
I think you'll find that most of them will tell you
that they "get it," then when you ask them to
explain it to you, you'll quickly realize that
they're confusing chaos with randomness.

See ch. 52, "A Higher
Level of Order."

Business Topology wasn't covered in either of my
first two books. It will be in Book Three, Magical
Worlds of the Wizard of Ads.

No, the APE is a statement of relationship, like $E = mc^2$.
It doesn't involve Business Topology. Look through
your Academy notebook handouts for the WizardSword
definition of Business Topology. I think you'll find
what you're looking for.

See ch. 27, "Business
Problem Topology."

CISNA offers a good definition of the Duality
Principle which I've reduced to about one eighth of
its original length for you, but it's still pretty

lengthy: "The scientific debate over whether light was a particle or a wave became rather heated because it cannot be both. Yet it is easily proven that light is both a wave and a particle. Light as a particle lies at the foundation of quantum mechanics. Light as a wave underlies Einstein's theory of general relativity. One rarely learns an operation in mathematics without also learning its inverse operation. Addition and subtraction, multiplication and division, the distributive law and factoring come to mind immediately as dual operations. Calculus is nothing more than the application of two dual operators that, in fact, are inverses of each other, integration and differentiation. In physics, action and reaction, positive and negative charges, particle and wave theories are known as dual principles. In economics, supply and demand, profit and loss are connected in a dualistic manner. In biology, inhaling and exhaling, the functions of chlorophyll and hemoglobin, muscle contraction and extension, osteoblasts and osteoclasts are known to have opposite functions. In philosophy and political science, the concepts of liberalism and conservatism and thesis vs. antithesis are examples of dualistic relationship. Mind and matter, space and time, subjective perception and objective reality, good and evil, yin and yang, light and dark, opportunity and security, the list is endless."

My use of the term "duality principle" in Wizard Academy is mostly to underscore the tension that exists in every 2nd-dimensional reality, that realm of rules -- "correct and incorrect". This tension is neatly resolved in 3rd-dimensional reality -- the realm of principles, faith and imagination. Duality tension again raises its ugly head to annoy us in 4th dimensional reality, our objective, space-time continuum. The realm of 2nd and 4th dimensional realities is left-brain. The right brain is where 1st and 3rd dimensional realities are experienced.

See ch. 10, "Waxing Woo-Woo."

"Now that I know who you are, I know who I am."
— Samuel L. Jackson to his nemesis, Bruce Willis, in *Unbreakable*

Have a great weekend, Wolfgang. And good luck with the staff where you work. (I think you may find that they don't see nearly so clearly as your wife.)

Yours,

Roy H. Williams

CC cjamesmaddock@aol.com

The size of the villain determines the size of the hero. Without Goliath, David is just some punk throwing rocks.

Billy Crystal in *My Giant*

16

The Neurology of Branding

eople who refer to the earth as round are technically wrong, but directionally accurate. Technically, our planet is an oblate spheroid. But to explain that subtle difference just wouldn't be worth the trouble, so we usually say, "The earth is round," and leave it at that. Likewise, what you are about to read is technically wrong, but directionally accurate.

For each of our senses, the brain offers short-term and long-term memory. Short-term memory is electrical. Long-term memory is chemical.

The objective of "branding" is to cause your product to be the one customers think of first and feel the best about when their moment of need arises. Therefore, branding must be accomplished in long-term memory.

You say, "No problem, it's just a matter of repetition, right?"

Wrong. The brain, you see, is a very smart organ. It knows better than to transfer data into long-term memory when that data is flashing a "soon-to-expire" message in neon letters.

Sleep is the eraser of electrical memory. As the mind is purged each night, the memories that are the most quickly and completely erased are those that are no longer relevant.

No ad with a deadline is relevant after the deadline has passed.

When an advertiser insists on trying to "whip people into action" with the urgency of a limited-time offer, he can be certain that his message will never make it into long-term memory. At best, the message will stay in short-term memory only until the expiration date has passed, and then it will be forever erased from the brain. Consequently, you cannot make a series of limited-time offers and call it a "branding" campaign.

SOME OF US RESPOND TO "BRANDING" BY VOWING NEVER TO BUY THE BRAND. PLEASE... TRY NOT TO MAKE YOUR AD OFFENSIVE. —JEFF MORRIS, EDITOR

The bottom line is that you can't have your cake and eat it, too. So which kind of advertising will you do? Short-term or long-term? Will you have a little piece of cake right now, or a series of larger pieces later on? This is the choice every advertiser makes, either consciously or unconsciously. I want you to make it consciously.

Yes, limited-time offers, when they work, cause people to take action immediately. The downside is that limited-time offers don't work better and better as time goes by. In truth, they work worse and worse. When an advertiser makes a limited-time offer, the only thing that goes into long-term memory is "This advertiser makes limited-time offers." In essence, that advertiser is training his customer to ask, "When does this go on sale?"

Will you invest your ad dollars in a long, slow, tedious branding campaign that will work better and better as time goes by? Or will you do short-term, high-impact, grab-for-the-brass-ring advertising and hope for a quick-hit payoff?

Will you bet on the tortoise or the hare?

See ch. 43, "BrandingBrandingBranding."

CLEATORS PROFITS TO BE THROWN TO THE BUYING PUBLIC
A Sensational Unparalled Stupendous Footwear Event
THE ENTIRE STOCK TO BE SOLD
Thousands of Dollars Worth of the Best Shoes ever brought into this City To be Sold at Incomparable Prices that will Shatter all Bargain Records

CLEATORS SHOE STORE

17

Why Do My Fingers Know This Song?

hy do my fingers know this song so much better than my mind?" is a question that's been asked by every piano player who ever played. Most recently, it was asked by Monica Ballard's mom. Monica answered, "I don't know, Mom, but I'll ask Roy tomorrow when I get to the office." Want to hear something funny? If Monica had asked me the question two days earlier, I wouldn't have known the answer, but as fate would have it, I had just finished researching that very subject.

Basically, there are three kinds of memory: working, declarative, and procedural.

Working memory is active memory, the thought that you are thinking now. It is imagination, the ability to see possibilities in your mind. Electrical and temporary, it is the RAM in the human computer.

Declarative memory is stored memory, all the things that you can remember. It is the recall of known information from the hard drive of your brain. Declarative memory is largely chemical.

Procedural memory is muscular memory, engraved into the very fabric of your being. It is instinctive and automatic, deeply embedded through much repetition. As I'm sure you've already guessed, Monica's mom was recalling the song through procedural memory.

But don't think of these categories of memory as isolated from one another. They overlap continually. You're swinging a baseball bat. You're consciously focused on how you're going to swing it; working memory (imagination) is involved. You're recalling the tips and rules you've memorized for swinging the bat correctly; that's your declarative memory. And when your muscles respond the same way they've done in your previous 1,000 swings, you're using procedural memory.

It's interesting to note that false memories are often implanted when an abstract, right-brain working memory (imagination) interacts with a left-brain (experience-based), declarative memory. This was recently demonstrated by University of Washington researchers Jacquie Pickrell and Elizabeth Loftus. They asked 120 people who had recently visited Disneyland to evaluate proposed advertising copy and answer questions about their trips. Among the ads these volunteers were asked to evaluate was a print ad describing how visitors to Disneyland could meet and shake hands with Bugs Bunny. Fully one-third of the 120 later described in detail how they clearly remembered seeing or meeting Bugs Bunny during their trip. Such an event, however, could not possibly have happened. Bugs Bunny is a Warner Brothers cartoon character and has never appeared at a Walt Disney property.

According to Jacquie Pickrell, "Creating a false memory is a process." You may not have had a great experience the last time you visited Disneyland or McDonald's, but since their ads give you the impression that you had a wonderful time, they can actually create that memory. "If advertising can get people to believe they had an experience that they never actually had, that is pretty powerful."

Amen, Jacquie, amen.

18

Will You Photograph or Paint?

In 1839, Louis Daguerre captured reality and presented it to an awestruck world on a silver-plated copper plate. Thirty years later, it was the rising popularity of this "photography" that moved Claude Monet to strike back with his own counterblow: a daring expansion of reality in blazing colors, a painting called *Impression Sunrise*. It soon became the stated goal of Claude Monet, Auguste Renoir, Berthe Morisot, Camille Pissarro, Paul Cezanne, Edouard Manet, and Edgar Degas "to capture an image that the camera could not."

The art world responded by calling their works "the art of lunatics and maniacs." In reviewing an Impressionist exhibition in 1871, the art critic for *Le Patrie* wrote, "In seeing the lot you burst out laughing, but with the last ones you finally get angry. And you are sorry you did not give the franc you paid to get in to some poor beggar." Speaking of these same Impressionist paintings today, art appraiser Lance Hermus tells us, "These works fetch, by far, the highest prices in the market. Even works of lesser quality sell in the millions."

It is profoundly sad to note that there was never an American Impressionist; not a single, solitary one. We Americans, you see, tend to stick to the facts. Following his visit to America in 1882, a right-brained Oscar Wilde wrote,

> The male American is the most abnormally serious creature who ever existed. He talks of Europe as being old; but it is he himself who has never been young. . . . He has always been prudent, always practical, and pays a heavy penalty for having committed no mistakes. It is only fair to admit that he can exaggerate; but even his exaggeration has a rational bias. It is not founded on wit or fancy; it does not spring from any poetic imagination.

Would Oscar Wilde have said what he said if he had met you? In your descriptions, are you of the tedious, posed school of Daguerre, or are you of the luminous school of Monet? Do you merely capture reality with your words, or do you expand it with colorful boldness in perceptual reality? ❧

If you are thinking, "Weren't Childe Hassam and Mary Cassat both American Impressionists?" then you have missed the Wizard's point entirely. "At first impression," most people cannot think of an American Impressionist. Thus, in his essay, the Wizard has provided us with an illustration of the very thing that he was writing about.
— Chris Maddock

Imagination was given to man to compensate him for what he is not, and a sense of humor was provided to console him for what he is.

Unknown

49

19

The Tollbooth
on the Yellow Brick Road

You are an advertising message. Your hope is to arrive at the Emerald City, the prefrontal cortex of the human brain, that place where decisions are made in the mind.

But a journey to the Emerald City is both long and difficult. Located just behind the forehead, the prefrontal cortex is isolated from all the parts of the brain that gather information from the outside world.

Good news: there is a Yellow Brick Road, a highway that will take you directly there!

Bad news: the only entrance to the Yellow Brick Road is through a tollbooth called Broca's area. Will you be able to pay the toll? "Interest me!" cries Broca. "Surprise me with something I didn't know. If you're not carrying new information or a new perspective, you'll not enter my Yellow Brick Road."

Although it's positioned next to the ear, Broca's tollbooth screens not just auditory data, but most types of neural information. Sight, sound, taste, pain, pressure, position, movement, and temperature are gathered and processed in various outlying areas of the brain, but all must pass through Broca's tollbooth on their way to the prefrontal cortex. Sitting in his tollbooth, Broca attaches verbs to actions as he anticipates the predictable. Broca turns away everything that he "sees coming."

Broca hates the predictable.

According to Dr. Alan Baddeley, director of the Medical Research Council Applied Psychology Unit at Cambridge, the Yellow Brick Road that runs between Broca's tollbooth and the Emerald City is called the "dorsolateral prefrontal association area of the brain," and it's a road that Dr. Baddeley calls "working memory."

You and I call it imagination.

According to Dr. Baddeley and his neurological associates, working memory (imagination) is composed of three parts: the central executive, the phonological loop, and the visuospatial sketchpad.

The central executive chooses where to direct your attention. After Broca has decided what does and doesn't matter, the central executive decides what matters most.

The phonological loop rehearses sound. Have you ever had a song get stuck in the phonological loop and you couldn't get it out of your head? The phonological loop (sometimes called the articulatory loop) is a cul-de-sac on the Yellow Brick Road.

The visuospatial sketchpad is where you "see" things that have never happened. Think of it as the movie screen of the mind.

Amazingly, all this happens on the Yellow Brick Road of the dorsolateral prefrontal association area, a part of your brain that is not connected to your eyes, but is attached directly to your ear. Sound is invasive, intrusive, and irresistible.

And there is no sound more seductive than the sound of words. Do you know how to use them? Can you pay your way past Broca's tollbooth? ❧

You can close your eyes, but you cannot close your ears. You hear when you are not listening. You hear even when you're fast asleep. (How else would you know when there's a burglar in the house?)

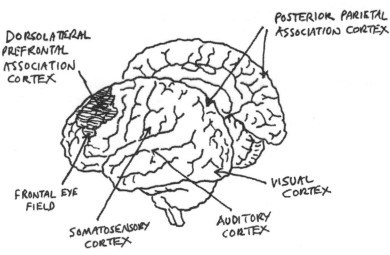

51

20

It's Party Time

May the name of Peter Gorner live forever, Amen.

On Monday, April 23, 2001, the *Chicago Tribune* published a story about the brain that I had waited four long years to read. In that story, the *Tribune's* Pulitzer Prize–winning science reporter, Peter Gorner, wrote:

> A study published Sunday in the journal *Nature Neuroscience* suggests for the first time that the rules of music may be processed in the same region of the left hemisphere located just above the ear, called Broca's area, that handles speech and language syntax. . . . "Music training is known to lead to enhanced verbal abilities and this may explain why," said psychologist Burkhard Maess, of the Max Planck Institute of Cognitive Science in Leipzig, Germany, who conducted the research.

When I saw these words, I lifted my face toward heaven and shouted, "Hallelujah!"

You may recall a chapter called "Surprising Broca" in my 1999 book, *Secret Formulas of the Wizard of Ads,* which said,

> Although none of the neurologists I've consulted can positively confirm or deny it, I am convinced that while a speaker uses Broca to arrange his words into understandable sentences, the listener uses Broca to anticipate and discount the predictable. When your listener hears only what she has heard before, it's difficult to keep her attention. . . . When speaking or writing, visualize Broca's area as a theater stage upon which your play will be performed in the listener's mind, and think of Broca as a theater critic — the judge who will determine whether or not to walk out on your play. If

you will present your play on this mental stage and gain the smiling approval of the judge, you must electrify Broca with the thrill of the unexpected.

For more than four years I've taught that the Emerald City of human persuasion is the prefrontal cortex (the part of the brain responsible for decisions, planning, and judgment), and that Broca's area is the all-important tollbooth at the entrance to the Yellow Brick Road (the dorsolateral prefrontal association area), and that the toll required at Broca's tollbooth is surprise — specifically, unpredictable words in unusual combinations. To say the least, I've endured a great deal of criticism from those who have conducted Internet keyword searches and have been unable to find anything about Broca's area anticipating the predictable. My response to their indignant e-mail demands for documentation has been flimsy at best: "I never read it. It was not taught to me. Can a man not speak the truth without quoting someone else?"

For those who are wondering exactly how Burkhard Maess and his colleagues at the Max Planck Institute bailed me out, allow me to explain. Using magnetoencephalography, Maess scanned the brain signals of a number of musically naïve volunteers while a series of chord sequences was played. When the volunteers heard a chord that was musically unrelated to the others — one that did not belong — a stronger magnetic field than usual was measurable in their brains. "The magnetic field came from a region called Broca's area, which is thought to be involved in understanding complex language." (*Nature Neuroscience*, vol. 4, p. 540.) In other words, Broca was stimulated by that which was not anticipated.

Thank you, Peter Gorner. ⌘

21

Below Deck in a Storm at Sea

Ted pursued a Ph.D. in English literature at Oxford for a while, but dropped out when he decided that his studies were "astonishingly irrelevant." In 1950, Ted invented the word "nerd." In 1984 he won a Pulitzer prize.

After dropping out of Oxford, Ted worked nine years for Standard Oil as a designer of brochures. In the summer of 1936, he found himself below deck on the *MS Kungsbold,* listening to the rhythm of the ship's engines in a focused attempt to distract himself from a terrifying storm. To further distract himself, Ted began writing a nonsensical poem to the motor's pounding beat. "I was trying to keep my mind off the storm that was going on. This rhythm persisted in my head for about a week after I was off the ship and, probably as psycho-therapy, I began developing the theme." When his nonsensical poem was finally complete, Ted decided that instead of signing it with his real name, Theodor S. Geisel, he would use only his middle name. And as long as he was writing nonsense, he would give himself an honorary doctorate. And in a singular, magical moment worthy of all the pixie dust of Tinker Bell, the world's beloved "Dr. Seuss" was born.

"Although I knew nothing about children's books, it sounded pretty good, so I decided to get it published. It was rejected by twenty-eight publishing houses before the twenty-ninth, Vanguard Press, agreed to take a chance on bringing it out." The main reason given by the other publishing houses for rejecting Ted's book, *And to Think That I Saw It on Mulberry Street,* was that it was too different from the other children's books on the market.

By the time of his death in 1991, the forty-six books written and illustrated by Ted Geisel had sold more than 200 million copies and had been translated into twenty languages. Former Random House

See ch. 100+1, "Dr. Seuss on Writing for Children."

president Bennett Cerf once remarked, "I've published any number of great writers, from William Faulkner to John O'Hara, but there's only one genius on my authors list. His name is Ted Geisel."

What keys did Ted use to unlock the vaults of wild success?

Key 1: Ted surprised Broca's area of the brain by using unpredictable words in unusual combinations. In fact, Ted often made up his own words altogether.

See ch. 19, "The Tollbooth on the Yellow Brick Road."

Key 2: In mimicking the rhythm of the ship's engines, Ted created echoic retention in the phonological loop of working memory, located in the dorsolateral prefrontal association area of the brain. You can't get Ted's stories out of your head.

Key 3: Ted refused to pay attention to the established rules of his category: children's books. He dared to do what had not yet been proven to work.

Key 4: Instead of writing about what was, Ted wrote about what was not. He knew the public was more willing to believe fiction than nonfiction.

Now that you have all four of Ted's keys, why don't you do what he did? I can assure you that the keys still work and the vaults are right where they've always been. ❧

The improbable happens just often enough
to make life either disturbing or delightful.

William Feather

22

Psycho-Myth No. 9

Sometimes you think you have something in the bag, but the bag breaks.

— Ernie Banks

ooner or later, a person standing at a whiteboard is going to tell you that there are three kinds of people: "visual, auditory, and kinesthetic." This person will inform you that "visual" people are easily identified because they say things like "I see what you mean. I can picture that. I view it the same way." You'll then be told that you can recognize "auditory" people through their use of such phrases as "I hear what you're trying to tell me. Sounds good to me. Listen to what I'm saying." Last, you'll be taught that "kinesthetic" people are those who use phrases like "I grasp what you're saying. I feel what you're saying is wrong. I am touched that you care."

Although this tidy little theory is taught from coast to coast, you'll not find a molecule of scientific evidence to support it. In fact, the whole concept is utterly incongruent with all that is currently known about the architecture and functions of the human brain. Consequently, it came as no surprise to me when the opening line of the first booklet I was able to find on the subject said, "This booklet is written using the old adage 'Keep It Simple, Stupid' because you are too busy to read through a lot of psychological babble." In other words, "This is a groundless theory based on zero medical research."

A serious investigation of the preferences labeled visual, auditory, and kinesthetic reveals the entire V-A-K theory to be little more than the unfortunate mislabeling of preferences long known to exist among persons who are left-brain and right-brain dominant.

Those persons mislabeled "visual" do have a preference, but it's not so much for eyesight as for empirical certainty, a common attribute of those who are left-brain dominant. Likewise, persons with a preference toward right-brain "instincts and intuition" (as opposed to left-brain "facts") are easily mislabeled "auditory" since the world of right-brain intuition is that place where colorful, "auditory" words can blaze into an epiphany of intuitive understanding. Left-brain vs. right-brain dominance is a real phenomenon, but it has nothing whatsoever to do with sight vs. sound.

The mislabeling of "kinesthetic" people is even further off the mark, since those who enjoy tactile sensations (the "sensing" preference, in Myers-Briggs terminology) are not necessarily the same ones who will use affective terms: "I feel what you're saying is wrong. I am touched that you care." Such phrases as these are more likely to indicate an emotional "feeling" preference (Myers-Briggs again) as opposed to any tactile "feeling" preference that might possibly be labeled "kinesthetic."

See ch. 26, "Getting to Know Yourself."

Can one's choice of words give us insight into that person? Absolutely so. Does one's choice of words indicate how that person gathers, processes, stores, and relates data differently than the brains of other humans? Absolutely, positively not.

The visual-auditory-kinesthetic theory sprang into existence because lazy people demanded quick and simple bullets, nuggets, rules, steps, and systems rather than investing the time and energy required to gain real understanding. ❧

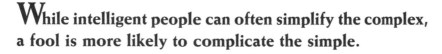

While intelligent people can often simplify the complex, a fool is more likely to complicate the simple.

Gerald W. Grumet

23

Same Whiteboard, Same Trainer...

ooms full of bright-eyed students coast to coast are being taught that "93 percent of all human communication is nonverbal." Tragically, these students often believe this absurdity and use it as an excuse for not learning how to become more compelling speakers and writers.

I wouldn't be quite so bothered if the whole "93 percent nonverbal" myth were just a cleverly constructed fraud, but it's actually worse than that. These sales trainers actually believe this stuff, though few of them can tell you why, other than to say, "It's what I was taught." Those who can "explain" will tell you that "55 percent of all communication is through body language and 38 percent is through voice tonality and only 7 percent is verbal."

Just add 55 percent to 38 percent and, voilà, you have 93 percent "nonverbal."

This whole "55-38-7" myth began when someone horribly misapplied an obscure comment from *Silent Messages,* a 1971 book by Dr. Albert Mehrabian. (The credit for this extraordinary detective work goes to Dr. C. E. Johnson, who provides the following details.) "From chapter 3 of *Silent Messages* we find that the numbers 7-38-55 expressed as percentages have to do only with what [Dr. Mehrabian] calls the resolution of inconsistent messages. . . . He also states that there are very few things that can be communicated nonverbally. . . . When I spoke with him by phone in March 1994, he stated that his findings and inferences were not meant to be applied to normal communications. They were of very limited application."

Following his conversation with Dr. Mehrabian, Dr. Johnson wrote, "Some people have made some rather sweeping and inaccurate generalizations. If we continue to disseminate erroneous information such as the 7-38-55 myth, I feel we are doing a grave disservice. . . . We could do a great service by helping the public realize that the words they use . . . are extremely important."

The simple truth is that words are the most powerful force there has ever been. I know it to be true, every cognitive neuroscientist in the world knows it to be true, and now, I hope, you know it, too.

There are lies, damned lies, and statistics.

Mark Twain

24

Did Your Valedictorian Get Rich?

The old assumptions — that intelligence and creativity are largely innate; that learning is strictly logical, objective and linear, and dependent on class time and the technology of pen, paper, and textbooks — are wrong. It is true that academic success involves largely solitary study, generally uninterrupted work, concentration on a single subject, and much writing. But commercial success — which depends equally on intelligence — involves understanding in many different disciplines, working with others, constant distractions, and mainly verbal skills.

> Employers are already saying that a degree is not enough, and that many graduates do not have the qualities they are looking for: the ability to communicate, work in teams, adapt to change, to innovate and be creative. This is not surprising. . . . The traditional academic curriculum is not designed to promote creativity. Complaining that the system does not produce creative people is like complaining that a car doesn't fly . . . it was never intended to. The stark message is that the answer to the future is not simply to increase the amount of education, but to educate people differently.
>
> — Professor Ken Robinson
> of the 21st Century Learning Initiative,
> a group of neuroscientists, psychologists,
> and educators committed to educational reform

> The factory was the inspiration for our current educational model. But America's old-fashioned factories are dead or dying and the limitations of America's traditional factory model of education have become manifest . . . and they are crippling.
>
> — Dr. Albert Shanker, President
> American Federation of Teachers, 1999

Get rid of that damn machine model. It's wrong. The brain is a biological system, not a machine. Currently we are putting children with biologically shaped brains into machine-orientated schools. The two just don't mix. We bog the school down in a curriculum that is not biologically feasible.

— Professor Robert Sylwester

It is, in fact, nothing short of a miracle that the modern methods of instruction have not yet entirely strangled the holy curiosity of inquiry; for this delicate little plant, aside from stimulation, stands mainly in need of freedom; without this it goes to rack and ruin without fail. It is a very grave mistake to think that the engagement of seeing and searching can be promoted by means of coercion and a sense of duty.

— Albert Einstein

What these people are saying, in a nutshell, is that America's system of education was built with a strong cultural bias toward the left hemisphere of the brain, the part that provides us with linear, sequential logic. Now neurologists are discovering that the right hemisphere, the intuitive, "artsy" half of the brain, is perhaps even more important to your success than the logical left side. ❧

"Everything was entirely memorized, yet nothing had been translated into meaningful words. The students were all sitting there taking dictation, and when the professor repeated the sentence, they checked it to make sure they wrote it down all right. Then they wrote the next sentence, and on and on. So you see, they could pass the examinations, and 'learn' all this stuff, and not know anything at all, except what they had memorized."

— Nobel laureate Prof. Richard Feynman, explaining the problems of left-brain-only education

See ch. 6, "Left, Right, Left, Right, Left, Right."

Mediocre men often have the most acquired knowledge.

Claude Bernard

61

25

But to Be Fair...

In this book, I have chosen to affirm the right-brain perspective only because right-brain contributions are so often minimalized in a society that is dominated by left-brain types. This is certainly not to imply that the left-brain "realistic" perspective is not valuable. The real truth is that it takes both left-brain and right-brain insights, as the following will illustrate:

Sherlock Holmes and Dr. Watson went on a camping trip. After a good meal and a bottle of wine they lay down for the night and went to sleep. Some hours later, Holmes awoke and nudged his faithful friend. "Watson, look up and tell me what you see." Watson replied, "I see millions and millions of stars." "What does that tell you?" asked left-brained Holmes. Right-brained Watson pondered for a moment. "Astronomically, it tells me that there are millions of galaxies and potentially billions of planets. Astrologically, I observe that Saturn is in Leo. Horologically, I deduce that the time is approximately a quarter past three. Theologically, I can see that the universe is magnificent and that we are small and insignificant. Meteorologically, I suspect that we will have a beautiful day tomorrow. What does it tell you?" Holmes was silent for a minute, then spoke. "Watson, you idiot. Someone has stolen our tent."

A right-brain definition:

cynic *n.* a villain whose faulty vision causes him to see things as they are, not as they ought to be.

Romanticism and science are good for each other. The scientist keeps the romantic honest and the romantic keeps the scientist human.

Tom Robbins

26

Getting to Know Yourself

e're going to discuss preference profiling. Uh-oh, I can already hear you thinking, "But it's just not right to pigeonhole people. You shouldn't put people in boxes."

I agree. And that's not what we're doing here.

Let me begin by clarifying what preference tests cannot do. (1) They cannot measure such things as honesty, morals, or mental illness. In other words, it is impossible for a preference profile test to reveal anything "bad" about you. (2) Preference profiling does not measure your abilities. These tests are not an indicator of what you can or cannot do.

See ch. 22, "Psycho-Myth No. 9."

So what use are the tests?

Used correctly, preference profiling is a marvelous tool for promoting harmony and reducing friction. Properly administered and interpreted, a preference profile will help you understand why you are valuable and how you can best contribute to the success of your team. When you and your co-workers understand one another's preferences, friction is reduced, harmony is amplified, and effectiveness is accelerated. You can relate to those around you and "do unto others the way they prefer to be done unto." (Any other use of preference profiling is, in my opinion, ill advised.)

The ancient Greek Hippocrates was the first to notice that people seemed to fall into one of four groups. He labeled these groups Sanguine, Choleric, Phlegmatic, and Melancholic. Although Hippocrates' basic observations were correct, his explanations for why people had these preferences was a little wacky.

Essentially, a preference profile measures personal preferences that loosely correspond to left-brain and right-brain dominance in four different areas:

1. **Energy:** Where do you charge your batteries? Extraverts (E) draw energy from the outside world of people and activities, Introverts (I) from an internal world of ideas and impressions.

Left Brain	Right Brain
Extraversion (E) (49.2% of pop.)	Introversion (I) (50.8% of pop.)
sociability	territoriality
breadth	depth
external	internal
interaction	concentration
energy expenditure	energy conservation
multiple relationships	limited relationships

2. **Attention:** What do you notice? Sensing (S) individuals gather "concrete and actual" information through the five senses: they see, hear, taste, touch, smell. Intuitive types (N) gather information through a "sixth sense" and notice what "might be."

Left Brain	Right Brain
Sensing (S) (73.3% of pop.)	Intuition (N) (26.7% of pop.)
experience is the teacher	ideas are the teacher
concrete	abstract
perspiration	inspiration
actual	possible
fact	fiction
practicality	ingenuity
sensible	imaginative

3. **Decisions:** Do you go with your head or your heart? Thinkers (T) organize information objectively and logically, Feeling (F) people in a subjective, value-oriented way.

Left Brain	Right Brain
Thinking (T) (40.5% of pop.)	Feeling (F) (59.5% of pop.)
impersonal	personal
justice	mercy
categorize	harmonize
critique	appreciate
analysis	sympathy
laws	extenuating circumstances
firmness	persuasion

4. Organization: Are you planned or spontaneous? Judgment (J) indicates a preference for living an organized life with no "loose ends"; Perception (P), for living a spontaneous life with unlimited options.

Left Brain	Right Brain
Judging (J) (54.0% of pop.)	Perceiving (P) (46.0% of pop.)
decide	gather more data
fixed	flexible
plan ahead	improvise
bring closure	keep options open
decision making	treasure hunting
decisive	tentative
urgency	plenty of time

Intuitive-Feeling (NF) people, above all, must be authentic. They must find their unique identity and live their lives as an expression of it. For them, integrity means the unity of inner self with outer expression.

Sensing-Perceiving people (SP) need to feel free to act. For them, "doing" is its own reward. They prefer to be impulsive, free spirits. Carpe diem!

Sensing-Judging people (SJ) need to belong. They often feel that they must earn a place of belonging by being useful, fulfilling responsibilities, being of service, giving to and caring for others instead of receiving from them.

Intuitive-Thinking people (NT) seek competence in themselves and others. They want to understand and control life. Driven by curiosity, the NT is often preoccupied with learning twenty-four hours a day.

The four profiles above, as described by the Myers-Briggs Type Indicator are four "types" that loosely correspond to those of

Hippocrates (Sanguine, Choleric, Phlegmatic, Melancholic)

Kolb (Diverger, Assimilator, Converger, Accommodator)

Jung (Feeler, Thinker, Sensor, Intuitor)

Keirsey (Idealists, Rationals, Guardians, Artisans)

Lowry (Blue, Orange, Gold, Green)

Bolton (Amiable, Analytical, Driver, Expressive)

Special thanks to Richard Grant, Ph.D., for his assistance with this chapter. ❧

It takes a lot of people to hold a civilization together; some of us are only here to ask the right questions.

Larry Niven

Part the Second

Tools for Profitable Persuasion

In Which the Wizard Produces the Means of Using the Unique Capabilities of Your Mind to Best Effect

The Seven Laws
of the Advertising Universe
(Whence Cometh the Power of Ads to Work Magic)

An Energy of Words has existed since the day He said, "Let there be light." Learn how to use this energy. You are created in His image.

Masses of People are predictable, though an individual person is not. The exception does not disprove the rule.

Intellect and Emotion are partners who do not speak the same language. The intellect finds logic to justify what the emotions have decided. Win the hearts of the people, their minds will follow.

Time and Money are two sides of a single coin. No person gives you his money until he has first given you his time. Win the time of the people, their money will follow.

Sight and Sound function differently in the mind, with sound being the surer investment. Win the ears of the people, their eyes will follow.

Opportunity and Security are inversely proportionate. As one increases, the other must decrease. High returns are gained from low-risk strategies only through the passage of time. He who will cheat time must embrace the risk of failure.

Engage the Imagination, then take it where you will. Where the mind has repeatedly journeyed, the body will surely follow. People go only to places they have already been in their minds.

27

Business Problem Topology

There is nothing new under the sun. Is there anything of which one can say, "Look! This is something new"? It was here already, long ago; it was here before our time.

— Solomon, in Ecclesiastes 1

hings have become stagnant and tedious. Your business needs a revolution, and you feel hot, revolutionary blood pounding through your veins. You don't know what to change, how to change it, or even where to start looking. The only things you know for sure are (1) you want to grow; (2) you've been banging your head on this invisible glass ceiling for far too long; and (3) you don't want to risk losing everything.

Congratulations. You're face to face with the classic Opportunity/Security Conundrum. If you want to start a revolution, you're going to have to do what's never before been done in your industry. And tall opportunity always comes with short security: "It's never been done before. . . . It's never been done before. . . ."

You'll recall that Law 6 of the Seven Laws of the Advertising Universe reads thusly: "Opportunity and Security are inversely proportionate. As one increases, the other must decrease. High returns are gained from low-risk strategies only through the passage of time. He who will cheat time must embrace the risk of failure."

Solid experience is the teacher of the left brain; creative ideas rule the right. Symbolic thinking is the bridge that connects the two, giving us access to the best of both worlds.

Law 6, the Opportunity/Security Conundrum, is like the law of gravity; it doesn't go away. But we routinely flout the law of gravity by observing the law of aerodynamics. Might symbolic thinking

Use symbolic thinking to defeat the Opportunity/Security Conundrum.

provide us with a similar "law of aerodynamics" that would allow us to shorten time and minimize risk without lowering potential high return?

Using symbolic thinking, we're going to apply the science of topology to business problems. So what is the shape of your problem? What are its defining characteristics? Solomon said there was nothing new under the sun. You can be certain that countless others have faced problems similar in shape to the one that faces you. How did they overcome those problems? To create a revolution, you're going to have to do what's never before been done — in your industry. But if you are wise, you'll borrow a technique that has already been tested, proven, and thoroughly refined in a parallel but unrelated industry.

Henry Ford didn't invent the automobile; that was done by Gottlieb Daimler and Karl Benz in 1886. Henry built his first car ten years later, at a time when more than 2,000 other backyard mechanics, equally as talented and hard-working as Henry, were also building cars. All of these 2,000 would-be carmakers were faced with the same, identical problem, and, as is the case in most industries, all 2,000 of them took great comfort in knowing that "everyone else has the same problem."

The problem facing Henry Ford and 2,000 other turn-of-the-century automakers was that an expert mechanic with a vast array of tools was needed to build a single car. The mechanic first had to build a frame; then axles, wheels, and suspension components; then an engine, transmission, chassis, and interior. There was no way to get around the need for a large number of expert mechanics who were each skilled in the use of a vast array of tools; no way to shorten the time required to complete each step of the process.

Henry Ford applied business problem topology to the problems of auto making and became one of the world's wealthiest people as a result. As you know, what separated Henry Ford from the other 2,000 mechanics was his use of the assembly line. But contrary to what you

topology (to·pol'·o·gy) *n.* the science of categorization according to shape or configuration. For example, the topology of a network shows the pattern in which the computers are interconnected. Common network topologies are the star, bus, and Token ring.

were taught in school, Henry didn't invent the assembly line. He borrowed it from a parallel but unrelated industry.

Henry looked at his need for an army of expert mechanics and wondered, "Where do Chicago meat packers find the thousands of skilled butchers they need to maximize the yield from each of the thousands of carcasses they process each day? Do they have some kind of accelerated training program? Certainly it takes an expert butcher all day to process just one animal."

Henry went to Chicago to visit a meat-packing plant and immediately upon his arrival saw that all the animal carcasses were hung on an overhead rail and moved along from butcher to butcher, each butcher cutting off an individual piece of meat in a dis-assembly line. It was a continuous flow of production using average men, each standing in one spot and holding a single tool. Henry asked, "How long have you guys been processing meat this way?" "Gee, I don't know," came the answer. "This is how everyone has done it for years."

Henry Ford instantly saw how he could reverse the dis-assembly process to solve his car construction problem. He went home and began drawing plans for the frames of cars to move on a conveyor belt from one work station to the next, with each worker adding a single part to the car. Standard procedure in one industry became a world-shaking revolution in another.

Henry Ford discovered the innovation model he needed at a meat-packing plant in Chicago.

Where will you find yours? 🙰

"Real commitment to customer service begins with real commitment to your employees."
— Bill Dahm, Mike's Express Car Wash

Why am I quoting a guy who washes cars? Because his family-owned chain of car washes in Indianapolis, Ft. Wayne, and Cincinnati leads the nation in employee retention, customer satisfaction, and profitability. Ever been to Indianapolis?

28

Parallel, But Unrelated

Human beings know a lot of things, some of which are true, and apply them. When we like the results, we call it wisdom.

— Herbert Simon

Business problem topology (BPT) sounds great in principle, you say, but how do you put it into practice? Easy as one two three, I say. (Later I'm going to advise you to regard numbered lists skeptically, but here's one you might actually find useful.)

Step 1: Find a parallel but unrelated business that has a problem with similar defining characteristics to the problem for which you would like to develop an innovation model.

Step 2: Look at how the parallel business overcame the problem.

Step 3: Adapt its solution to solve your own business problem.

The first time I ever taught BPT at Wizard Academy, a student on the front row said, "Well, that might work for manufacturers and retailers and such, but I own radio stations and there's no parallel business for that."

"Well, then, maybe Solomon was wrong," I said, "and there is something new under the sun after all. Maybe you are actually faced with a problem no one has ever had before. But before we go that far, let's take a look at its defining characteristics."

"Here's the defining characteristic of the radio business," he said. "There is nothing worth less than yesterday's unsold inventory. At the stroke of midnight, today's unsold ads will vanish forever, never to return. They're gone, gone, gone. But whether all of today's ads are sold or none of today's ads are sold, the cost of running the radio station remains the same."

See ch. 13, "Four Kinds of Thought, Three Kinds of People."

"Yeah, that's a problem," I said. "I can't think of any other business that faces the problem of disappearing inventory. But maybe when you go back to your hotel room tonight, something will occur to you. Or maybe something will come to you as you sit down in the airplane that's going to fly you back home."

Just then, one of the other students spoke up. "Isn't the cost of running a hotel about the same whether all the rooms are rented or none of the rooms are rented? Doesn't it cost an airline about the same to fly a jet whether all the seats are sold or none of the seats are sold? What about movie theaters, concert promoters, and hospitals? How do they deal with the problem?"

An interesting question, wouldn't you say? And if our radio friend proves diligent enough to investigate, I'll wager that one of the answers will trigger a low-risk, high-return revolution solution.

When creating the curriculum for Wizard Academy, I faced a similar challenge: "How can I teach revolutionary, unheard-of techniques in human persuasion that have already been tested, proven, and refined?" I found my answer through a simple exercise in BPT.

Defining Characteristic of Wizard Academy: "We want to teach human persuasion. We want to teach our students how to change the way people think and feel. We want to teach time-tested techniques for effectively transferring a new perspective."

Can you think of anyone not in the business of advertising or education whose objective was to change how people think and feel?

How about prize-winning photographers like Robert Frank? How about legendary painters like Claude Monet and Pablo Picasso? Novelists like Ernest Hemingway and Tom Robbins? Poets like Robert Frost and Jack Kerouac? Composers of music like Amadeus Mozart and Paul Simon? Did any of them ever explain the techniques they used to change how people think and feel?

Yes, as a matter of fact, they did.

Keep reading. The best is yet to come. ꙮ

WizardSwords:

business problem topology (BPT): the practice of identifying parallel business problems by matching their defining characteristics.

defining characteristics: unusual features or distinguishing elements which are used to identify the "shape" of a business problem.

parallel business: in BPT, a business whose solutions to problems are studied in an effort to discover a portable innovation model.

29

Quick Miracles

You're a wounded soldier in unbearable pain during WWII, so the medics give you a shot of morphine. When your pain returns, they give you another shot. Morphine erases pain. So, as long as the medics don't run out of morphine, that's the end of your problem, right?

Not quite. You're still wounded, remember? The morphine is merely masking your symptoms. What you really need is life-saving surgery and a time of rehabilitation.

So what should I pull out of my bag right now, Soldier? My surgical tools, the solution to your problem? Or morphine, that tasty little drug that takes away the pain while you bleed and die?

What's that you say? A pill that will make the pain go away and heal the wound, like you were never wounded at all? Sorry, that pill doesn't exist. What's your second choice?

Pain is your body's warning to your conscious mind: Hey, Genius, we have a problem that requires your immediate attention. Business pain works the same way. Every businessperson in financial pain needs to understand the following:

- Your business is telling you it has a problem that requires your immediate attention.
- "Slow traffic" or a "downward sales trend" is not the problem, but merely a symptom of it.
- At best, every fast-acting ad gimmick is a painkiller exactly like morphine.
- Morphine quickly becomes addictive, and if you use it too long, it will kill you.
- No one looks forward to the surgeon's knife, even when it's what he or she desperately needs.

- Because of their woefully incomplete training, most advertising people are not equipped to perform life-saving surgery, but are outfitted merely as medics to promote their own proprietary brand of morphine.
- Recovery from life-saving surgery is painful, slow, and not the least bit fun.
- Playing with morphine, cocaine, heroin, and other painkillers is hysterical fun!

Are you beginning to understand why businesspeople are drawn to fast-acting ad gimmicks whenever they're in financial pain? Making morphine is easy, but using it is dangerous, and often deadly.

Now that I've plainly and coldly warned you of its insidious nature and highly addictive, seductive, and deadly properties, I'll teach you "How to Make Business Morphine." Read on.

More Than Aspirin

In an effort to eliminate the addictiveness of morphine, German pharmacists tinkered with its molecular structure and in 1874 invented a derivative of it called diacetylmorphine. In 1898, the Bayer Company named the derivative "Heroin." (In associative memory, the name conjures the image of a beautiful feminine hero. We're talking about branding here, kids.) Bayer marketed Heroin as a less addictive and less toxic alternative to morphine. Since Heroin was merely a premetabolized version of morphine, it was faster acting and more powerful than morphine; it went directly to the brain. It was also a lot more addictive. Heroin wasn't made illegal until 1924. Now we've really got a headache.

30
How to Make Business Morphine

Strap in. I'm taking you on a high-speed chase down a one-way road to nowhere. I'm going to teach you how to scam, flim-flam, and deceive your way to riches. I'm teaching you to do this, not because I believe you should do it, but so you'll be able to recognize it, look it in the eyes, and call it by name.

Sigh. It's confession time.

I dropped out after just two days of college and took a job selling advertising on straight commission. In other words, if I didn't sell enough this week, Pennie and I didn't eat enough next week. I learned much of what I know today by systematically spending millions of dollars of other people's money on a series of idiotic experiments and then carefully analyzing the results. Believe me, I got an incredibly expensive education; I just wasn't the one who had to pay for it.

On the streets I learned that most business owners see advertising as a giant gumball machine. "You puts in your money, you cranks the handle, and out comes the result. That's advertising." So I offered these business owners what they wanted — an instant miracle. I became the King of Hype, comparable only to Ron Popeil of the "But wait! There's more!" Veg-O-Matic. Joseph Bessemer spoke the truth when he said, "There's a sucker born every minute," because that's precisely how often I met one. (You thought P. T. Barnum said that? Nope, it was Joe Bessemer.) My employer required me to wear a tie, so I kept one draped around my neck, but I was careful never to tie it. I was Mr. Everywhere-in-a-Theater-Near-You. "You want a crowd? Crowds cost money, baby. How big a crowd do you want?" But I digress. I promised to teach you how to make morphine. . . .

Creating successful hype ads is simple. Here's all you need:

1. Intrusiveness. You've got to get their attention.

2. Offer. Make it too good to pass up.

3. Logic. Add supporting evidence to make doubters believe.

4. Urgency. There's got to be a time limit.

Leave out any of these ingredients, and you're dead in the water.

Having experienced the thrilling results of an intrusive offer made with logic and urgency, my advertisers instantly became morphine addicts, and I was their pusher. I'd waltz through their doors wearing my trademark tie like a scarf, and they'd say, "We sure had a great one last week, didn't we! What are we gonna do this week, huh? What have you got for me this week? What are we gonna do?" They'd bare their arms and I'd slip in the needle. But there is a law of the universe that says, "Anything that works quickly will work less and less well the longer you keep doing it," so my magic would always fade. And the bigger and faster our success, the quicker and more complete the fade.

No problem, there's a new sucker born every minute, right?

Sadly, most of the business owners who survived my abuse of them a quarter-century ago are still hoping that someday I'll return with the next "creative idea." (In the flim-flam business, "creative idea" was my preferred word for "gimmick.") Like all addicts, these business owners resisted taking the long view and continue to this very day to measure success on an extremely short time-horizon. Even when I tried to warn them that my "talk loud and draw a crowd" strategy was doing long-term damage to their business, they really didn't care.

Addicts never do. ೯෴

Your advertising plan should be precisely as long as your business plan. If you're promoting a concert that will be held on Wednesday night, then it would not be smart to buy advertising to run the following Thursday. The only thing that might be less smart would be to buy a 13-week advertising schedule for a business that plans to be around longer than 13 weeks.

A good ad is a seed for a fruit tree. Repetition is its water. Weekly consistency is its sunlight. The longer your seed is allowed to grow in the mind of the public, the greater and greater your harvests will be. What size harvests do you want to see?

31
Mitigating Morphine's Danger

ave you shouted "Sale!" so often that customers now ask your salespeople, "When will this go on sale?" Do you find it more and more difficult to sell products that aren't on sale? Do you have a business morphine habit you'd like to kick, but worry about the financial withdrawal pains?

A Harvard study on customer loyalty revealed the following three types of customers:

1. Nonswitchable. Nothing you can say or do will get these customers to switch from their current provider in your category.

2. Switchable. You can win these customers, but only if you say the right things and keep on saying them long enough. The goal of a "branding campaign" is to become the company these customers think of first and feel the best about when they need what you sell.

3. Switchable for reasons of price alone. These customers are easily won, but will switch from you just as quickly as they switched to you, and for the same reason. There's nothing that cannot be made a little worse and sold a little cheaper.

You'd like to begin branding your name in the better customer's long-term (chemical) memory instead of depending on a series of short-term (electrical memory) promotions targeted to the switchable-for-reasons-of-price-alone customer. But you're afraid to quit the short-term gimmicks because you're worried that you won't be able to survive the chickening-out period between seedtime and harvest, right? Another thing that worries you is how long it's been since you met anyone willing to pay full price. Down deep, you worry that all customers are coupon-clipping, grave-robbing, bargain-hunting predators who will never agree to buy from you unless they're convinced they're getting "the deal of a lifetime."

Bottom line: You have a history of attracting customers for reasons of price alone. So how can you now begin attracting better customers without losing the coupon-clipping grave robbers too soon?

Answer: Use a visual recall cue in a nonintrusive (silent) medium. Run a newspaper ad with a large picture of what's "On Sale!" but with your company's name buried in the fine print. The only people who will know it's your company having a sale will be those looking for your product. The newspaper's lack of intrusiveness, its principal weakness in long-term branding, now lets you advertise your Hurry! Hurry! Once in a Lifetime Sale "anonymously."

Humans don't see unless they're looking. The only people to notice the visual recall cue, the photo of your product, will be those looking to buy your product. But humans hear and retain information even when they are not listening, so above all, DO NOT use TV, cable, or radio ads to stimulate response to the newspaper ad. Unless, of course, you want to train everyone who is not now in the market to wait for your next sale.

During this newspaper-advertised "sale," allow your broadcast ads to continue building long-term brand awareness in the minds of the not-yet-in-the-market majority.

The downsides of this technique:

1. You can't get away with it forever. Keep it up, and soon you'll be right back where you started.

2. Because you will be maintaining two separate ad campaigns, your advertising costs will be way out of line throughout the three- to six-month period of transition.

3. It isn't painless and easy, it's painful and hard, because sometimes the newspaper ads don't pull.

But if you're truly committed to taking your company in a new direction, you will survive this difficult transition period and emerge from it more profitable, with more consistent customer traffic patterns and more stability throughout your customer base.

Good luck. And remember: One day at a time. Ꮨ

32

How's Your Gravity Well?

ales trainers who focus on "closing the sale" assume that the relationship between seller and buyer is adversarial, rather than one of mutual good. As a result, the selling style they teach is often offensive and demeaning, a canned series of loaded "trick 'em and stick 'em" questions designed to hustle the buyer into whatever the salesperson wants to sell. Is it any wonder that a mother rarely says of her little boy, "I hope he grows up to be a salesman"?

Great sales trainers like Chuck Mefford and Brad Huisken teach that a salesperson should aspire only to become the customer's servant, consultant, and friend; and having accomplished this, never to violate the terms of that friendship. Human persuasion is not a confrontation with each side trying to "win."

What a business wants is a committed customer. But a customer is far more likely to make a small commitment, or to increase an existing commitment by a small degree, than to make a large commitment abruptly. Commitment is rarely an all-at-once thing. Salespeople who ask for large commitments too soon are typically referred to as "pushy," and most people hate dealing with them.

Profitable persuasion and comfortable customer compliance are merely the results of a properly constructed gravity well. Have you ever charted your own gravity well? According to my good friend Phil Stewart, a properly constructed gravity well softly pulls, entices, and seduces the customer into gradually deeper degrees of commitment. But unlike the tricky "sales trap," the customer may comfortably exit the gravity well at any time.

Shaped like a funnel, the gravity well is most easily entered at the uppermost level, and requires only the mildest level of interest.

"Sales resistance" is what happens when the customer is asked to jump too deeply into the well, too quickly.

80

In this, the widest part of the funnel, your customers will be numerous but uncommitted.

Just inside the rim of my company's gravity well is the *Monday Morning Memo,* a weekly newsletter we send at no charge to subscribers around the world. Those who wish to delve deeper will buy one or more of my books, an investment of tens of dollars. At the next level, readers may opt to spend a few hours to attend a free seminar, or to purchase one of my video series for a few hundred dollars. Of these, a few will come to Austin to attend our three-day Wizard Academy and join an elite, inner circle of graduates. Finally, from the very tip of the funnel will trickle the occasional new client who asks to pay my firm tens of thousands of dollars per year in return for creating and guiding his ad campaign. ❧

But at no time in the process is anyone asked to buy anything. That's the elegance of a gravity well.

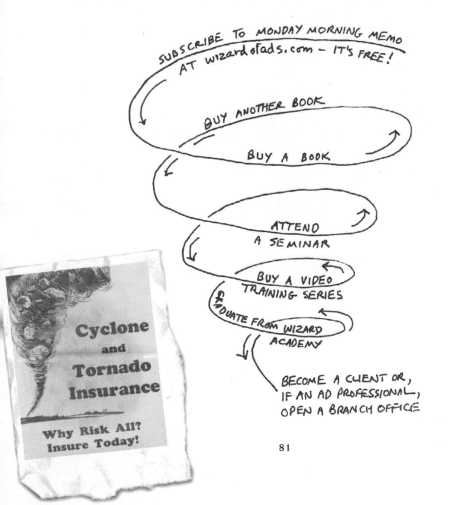

SUBSCRIBE TO MONDAY MORNING MEMO AT wizardofads.com — IT'S FREE!

BUY ANOTHER BOOK

BUY A BOOK

ATTEND A SEMINAR

BUY A VIDEO TRAINING SERIES

GRADUATE FROM WIZARD ACADEMY

BECOME A CLIENT OR, IF AN AD PROFESSIONAL, OPEN A BRANCH OFFICE

33

Share of Voice

 f all the advertising that is currently being done in your business category, how much of it is yours? Do you know your share of voice (SoV)?

In media terms, "reach" is the number of people that your advertising schedule will reach. "Frequency" is the number of times, on average, that your message will reach them. In other words, frequency is the media's term for repetition.

"During the day, many bits of information enter short-term memory, but most of it is unimportant and can be easily discarded. But other information is important, so the brain needs to meld it with older memories, storing the new information as it updates the older."

— Dr. Terence Sejnowski,
neuroscientist,
Salk Institute,
La Jolla, California

"The brain accomplishes this by entering a series of different chemical and electrical states during the day and night."

— Dr. Alexander Borbely,
University of Zurich
sleep researcher

If you run a television ad fifty times, how many of these ads will the typical viewer see? What will be the frequency? If you run a newspaper ad twelve times, how many times will the typical subscriber read it? What will be the frequency? If you run a radio ad 100 times, how many of these will the typical listener hear? What will be the frequency? Do you assume that every person who is reached just once or twice is fully and sufficiently "reached"? And how much time is elapsing between repetitions? Do you think it doesn't matter?

It is essential that advertisers be aware of their seven-day frequency because sleep erases advertising, a little bit each night, and human beings are programmed on a seven-day cycle.

You and I live in an overcommunicated society. Advertising messages relentlessly peck us and pelt us each day like ice balls in a hailstorm. Your customer lives in this same overcommunicated society. So it is far more effective today to reach fewer people with relentless frequency than to reach more people with little repetition.

It is important that you be aware of your share of voice.

Bad Math

Most stations have a computer loaded with the latest ratings information. A media sales rep need only press a few keys, and this computer will spit out the correct answer to whatever question it is asked. Unfortunately, most people are asking the wrong questions.

Advertising is bought and sold today using a system of "gross impressions" (GIs) and "gross ratings points" (GRPs). When the ratings computer is asked to calculate GIs, it immediately examines the latest survey data, multiplies reach times frequency, and then spits out the number of GIs that the schedule in question would yield. In other words, if the schedule's reach is 100,000 people and the frequency is 10, the computer will spit out "1,000,000 gross impressions." The computer will give you the same answer if your schedule were going to reach 1,000,000 people once, 100,000 people ten times, or 50,000 people 20 times. In all three instances, the computer would answer "1,000,000 gross impressions," and in a city of 1,000,000 people, that's exactly "100 GRPs." In other words, 1 GRP is earned by reaching the mathematical equivalent of 1 percent of the city, 1 time. One hundred GRPs is the mathematical equivalent of reaching 100 percent of the city 1 time, or 10 percent of the city 10 times, or 5 percent of the city 20 times. Are you beginning to see the problem? Only a fool would say that it doesn't matter.

Gross impressions and gross ratings points are bad math. Use these in making your media buying decisions, and you'll reach too many people with too little repetition. This is one of the major reasons most advertising in America today isn't working like it should.

Every time I warn a roomful of advertisers about the dangers of reaching too many people with too little repetition, I can always count on someone raising a hand to ask, "Just how much repetition is enough?" My answer is always the same: "On average, you need the same listener to hear the same radio or TV ad at least 3 times within 7 night's sleep, 52 weeks a year. The number of people you can afford to reach will be determined by your ad budget." To get this information from a ratings computer, you need only ask it to calculate a reach-and-frequency analysis that will show you exactly how many ads you'll need to run in one week, and at what times they'll need to run, for your budget to yield a 3 frequency each week with the maximum number of listeners. ᕙᕗ

WizardSwords

share of voice: your company's percentage of all the advertising done in your business category.

See "Hot Tip," p. 96 (chapter 39, "A Coiled Cobra Called 'Statistics'")

Reach is easily traded for frequency. Tightening the daypart (horizontal scheduling) is how it's done.

34

Impact Quotient

The impact quotient (IQ) of your message is its power to convince the customer. To what degree is your message relevant, or salient, to your customer? If the average ad in your product category scores an impact quotient of 1.0, what do your ads score? If they're 40 percent stronger than the average ad, your impact quotient is 1.4. If they're 10 percent less convincing than the average ad, you get a 0.9. Your impact quotient is measured against a marketplace average of 1.0.

Impact quotient, saliency, the relevance of your message to the customer, is the single most overlooked factor in advertising today.

The average message needed to be heard about three times a week, every week, to have a shot at being transferred from short-term, electrical memory to long-term, chemical memory. But that's the average message. The higher the impact quotient (saliency), the less repetition is required to store it. An off-the-chart impact quotient is why you can still remember exactly where you were when the O. J. Simpson verdict was announced, even though you heard it only once. Unfortunately, it's not likely that your advertising message will ever achieve this sort of impact quotient.

A strong ad with a smaller budget will beat a weak ad with a larger budget almost every time. The difference in the results of these ad campaigns is directly attributable to the difference in the impact quotients of their ads.

How strong is your impact quotient?

Good ad writers answer the telephone like teenage girls who have been waiting for their boyfriends to call. "Hello, hello, is it finally you?" What the writer will most likely hear is this: "I need some new ads. And make sure they're good ones." (Click)

WizardSwords

uncovery: an investigative effort to find an advertiser's unique and wonderful story; "digging for the diamond." Every worthy business has a story that is uniquely and wonderfully its own. The job of the ad writer is to "uncover" this story and tell it.

Sword in the Stone: the focal idea, the axis around which all else will revolve, the non-negotiable standard at the heart of the company; the North Star in the heart of the client.

Oh yeah, that's real inspiration. I'll bet we're going to see some really good ads now.

CEOs, if you haven't taken the time to convince your ad writers, how do you expect them to convince the world? Your sales job is a comparatively easy one. Your ad writers are anxious and their minds are open and they're willing to give you their undivided attention. Can the same be said for your customer, the person these ad writers need to reach?

Selling begins with the ad writers. If you own a business, selling your writers on your company is the single most important sale that you will ever make.

True selling is never based on pressure, deception, trickery, or gimmicks. True selling is nothing more, and nothing less, than a transfer of confidence. The job of an ad writer is to transfer confidence to your prospective customers. But how can your writers transfer what they do not have? Your ad writer needs to believe in you and in your company.

Are you making this most important sale?

Can you think of any other investment of your time that might yield as high a return? ᧬

According to a study conducted by Edison Media Research, time spent listening (TSL) dropped 14% among radio listeners between 18 and 24 years old and almost as much among listeners 12 to 17. Although these survey results paint a pretty grim picture of the future of radio, the good news is that the problem is easily solvable. You see, it wasn't surfing the Internet or playing video games or listening to CDs that caused TSL to decline among America's youth. Fully three-quarters of those surveyed listed "too many commercials" as their principal reason for not listening to the radio. But to say "The obvious solution is for stations to play fewer commercials" would be a tragic misinterpretation of the data. The solution is not to play fewer commercials, but to play better ones. American kids hate advertising because most of it is irrelevant and boring. The solution is to increase the impact quotient.

35

Share of Mind

The terms "share of voice" and "share of mind" are not interchangeable. The difference being that share of voice can be purchased, but share of mind must be earned. Share of voice is determined by your schedule in the media, but share of mind is the amount of mental real estate you own in the public's mind. Share of mind has at least as much to do with the impact quotient of your message as it has to do with your share of voice:

Share of Voice × Impact Quotient = Share of Mind

Let's say you have a long-term, 20 percent share of voice and your ads are 50 percent better than average for your product category, giving them an impact quotient of 1.5. Your share of mind in this case would be 30 percent.

If, however, your ads scored only 0.8 impact quotient, the resulting share of mind would be just 16 percent.

You could still earn a 30 percent share of mind, however. All you'd need to do is buy a 38 percent share of voice:

38% Share of Voice × 0.8 Impact Quotient = 30.4 Share of Mind

But which makes more sense to you? To spend a fortune flooding the media with weak ads, or to spend a little time raising your impact quotient?

In your brain, short-term memory is electrical. Long-term memory is chemical. Short-term, electrical memory is like the RAM in your computer. Long-term, chemical memory is like your computer's hard drive. If you want data to be "saved," it must be saved to the hard drive before you power down the computer.

WizardSwords

share of mind: an advertiser's percentage of the customer's total awareness in a product or service category.

The human computer is powered down once a day when we turn out the lights and crawl between the sheets. Most of what was in RAM (electrical memory) will be lost during the night. Sleep causes the information in electrical memory to fade according to its degree of "saliency," or relevancy. Data that is more important, or "salient," does not fade as quickly from the mind.

The only things you can do to increase the transfer of your message from electrical memory to chemical memory are (1) increase the saliency of the message, and (2) increase the frequency of its repetition (essentially, raise the impact quotient of your ads and/or increase your share of voice).

If your goal is to "brand" your product, you'll need a memorable message and sufficient weekly frequency. Do you have them? Branding is accomplished only when you have a salient message that is repeated with enough frequency to become securely stored in the hard drive of the brain. ❧

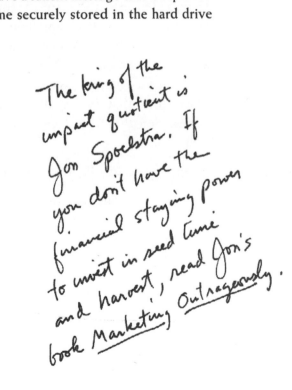

The king of the impact quotient is Jon Spoelstra. If you don't have the financial staying power to invest in seed time and harvest, read Jon's book Marketing Outrageously.

36

Personal Experience Factor

It is unusual to find a business owner who asks advertising to do only what it can. Most expect advertising to do what it cannot.

Let me say this plainly: Advertising cannot repair a broken business. It will not make you better at what you do. It cannot turn failure into success. Advertising will only accelerate what was going to happen anyway. When it comes to correcting the problems of poor selection, low quality, high prices, bad locations, lack of expertise, inconvenient hours, weak warranties, surly employees, shabby décor, and the negative word-of-mouth that flows from each of these, advertising is essentially impotent. But ask that struggling business owner why his business is in a slump, and he'll most likely say, "Our advertising isn't working. We're just not seeing enough traffic."

Think for a minute. You can name some very successful businesses in your town that do virtually no advertising, right? So why does it surprise you that a business can also struggle and fail in spite of brilliant ads?

Share of Mind × Personal Experience Factor = Share of Market

The world outside your door is the world of the customer's expectations. It's the world of impact quotient and share of voice; it's the world of advertising. But once the customer steps through your doorway, calls your phone number, or samples your product, she has moved from the world outside your door to the world inside your door. What will be her personal experience there?

If your business has what it takes to succeed, you can succeed in spite of bad advertising. But if you aren't good at what you do, or if people don't want to buy what you sell, then advertising will be just

---

WizardSwords

personal experience factor (PEF): an advertiser's reputation, through experience. Like the impact quotient, a PEF score ranges above and below an average of 1.0, with 1.0 being the expectations of the customer. The growth or decline of a company will ultimately follow that company's PEF as it rises and falls above and below 1.0.

one more bill you can't pay. (Ouch! It hurts to have to say such things, but we need to get the truth on the table.)

The personal experience factor, like the impact quotient, is measured against a 1.0. But this time we're not comparing the strength of your ads to your competitor's ads, we're measuring your customers' expectations to their actual experience with your company. If your customers walk out your door having had precisely the experience they expected, you score 1.0. If you fall short of their expectations by 25 percent, you score 0.75. If you exceed their expectations by 30 percent, your PEF is 1.3. Congratulations! You have a 30 percent "delight factor" going for you! You're going to be thrilled with how well your advertising pays off.

But a weak PEF can undo a whole lot of good advertising. Remember the 30 percent share of mind that we earned in the last chapter? Watch what happens to share of market when the advertiser delivers a PEF of 0.75:

30% Share of Mind × 0.75 PEF = 22.5% Share of Market

You probably think your company's PEF is pretty good — at least average, right? Let me warn you, that's exactly what people with extremely low PEF scores believe about their companies, too.

One day when I was struggling to figure out if my company had a story that was uniquely and wonderfully its own, my friend Mike Webb said to me, "It's hard to read the label when you're inside the bottle." So I began asking people "outside the bottle" what they saw. When I finally convinced them I wasn't going to be angry with them no matter what they told me, I was stunned by their clarity of vision. In fact, I'm still stinging from it, because while half of what they said made me feel great, the other half cut me to the heart. But the advice Mike gave me was wise.

And now I've given it to you. ❧

When you feel your advertising dollars aren't really performing for you, take a hard look at your impact quotient and your PEF. I guarantee that your problem is with one or both of them.

89

37

Market Potential

Share of Market × Market Potential = Sales Volume of Advertiser

At minus 459 degrees Fahrenheit — absolute zero — electrons freeze in their orbits around the nucleus of an atom. At the speed of light, time stands still. Mankind has never achieved either one of these.

And you're not going to sell 100 percent of your market potential.

When you've reached the sales altitude of about 33 percent of your market potential (MPo), you'll find that the air gets very thin and it gets harder and harder just to hang onto what you've got. And in all but the rarest circumstances, it's been my observation that there is a very real "speed of light" that cannot be exceeded — about 40 percent of market potential.

The advantage of the advertiser in a smaller market is that media are cheaper and share of voice is easier to get. The disadvantage is that there's also a much lower ceiling for growth.

Advertising dollars buy a proportionally smaller share of voice in a large market than in a smaller one. This puts enormous pressure on the impact quotient and PEF of the large-market advertiser, because these must compensate for his lack of budget. The advantage of being a large-market advertiser is that once you've finally achieved critical mass, you still have plenty of opportunity for growth. You don't have the problem of a low ceiling.

All other factors being equal, growth will start faster and end sooner in a smaller market than in a larger one.

Since our first client, Woody Justice, was a jeweler, we became very well known among jewelers when Woody began doubling and tripling his sales volume each year. (As you might expect, we soon

WizardSwords

share of market: an advertiser's percentage of the total business volume done in his business category.

market potential (MPo): the total dollars available in a business category.

had a couple of dozen jewelry-store clients and were becoming rather worried about our company being perceived as a "jewelry store specialist." But that's another story.) Three of these jewelers became close friends and made a friendly wager. Woody, in Springfield, Missouri, Robert, in New Orleans, and Richard, in Milwaukee, each pledged to pay $1,000 to whoever had the highest sales volume each year. When the wager began, all three had, with our help, already significantly increased their sales volume and were reasonably close together in gross sales.

I advised strongly against the wager, knowing that each year two of them would feel that my company had let them down. When all three refused to call off the bet, I said to Robert and Richard, "Okay, just please know that you're both going to be paying Woody $1,000 a year for the next few years, then Woody will have to start mailing money to one of you. My guess is that it will be Richard, because Robert is facing two really tough competitors in New Orleans."

The average jewelry store in the United States has a gross sales volume of less than $650,000 per year. After calculating the jewelry sales per capita for each of their states and multiplying it by the population in each marketplace, I told Woody he would probably collect money from Richard and Robert until he got to a sales volume of around $11 million a year. I told Richard and Robert that when they got to about $30 million a year, they would likewise have to learn to be content. Since each of them was doing only a couple of million dollars a year at the time, they all grinned like Cheshire Cats and said, "From your lips to God's ears!" I have to remind Woody of this when he starts moaning about the $1,000 that he has to send to Milwaukee or New Orleans each year.

I don't have the heart to tell them that Los Angeles jeweler Steve Robbins bit the bullet, grabbed for the brass ring, and is currently closing in fast on his personal target of $100 million a year. ✺

Remember what I said about big markets having a higher ceiling?

38

The APE

E=mc^2 is not a formula. You can't write it down on a sheet of paper, take it home, and calculate the answer. Albert's equation is merely a statement of the relationship between energy, mass, and the speed of light. Basically, it says that the inherent energy of a thing is equal to its mass times the speed of light times the speed of light.

Likewise, the APE — advertising performance equation — is not a formula. It's not a list of steps and rules. It's simply a "statement of relationship," similar to E=mc^2. But it's a very beautiful thing.

The triad of APE sub-equations looks like this:

Share of Voice × IQ = Share of Mind
Share of Mind × PEF = Share of Market
Share of Market × MPo = Sales Volume

Thus, the master equation reads,

SoV × IQ × PEF × MPo = Sales Volume

where

SoV = Share of Voice
IQ = Impact Quotient
PEF = Personal Experience Factor
MPo = Market Potential

The unfortunate truth, however, is that you can't measure your impact quotient, share of voice, or personal experience factor with any degree of accuracy. The APE statement of relationship remains true, nonetheless. It is the measurement of its individual components that's the tough part.

Specifically, the problems are these:

1. Utimately, share of voice is unique to the individual, as each person has different reading, listening, driving, and viewing habits, and is therefore exposed to different ads than his fellows. And will we measure share of voice for the past six months, one year, ten years, or fifty years? The percentages would change significantly with each new term of measurement.

2. Likewise, impact quotient is unique to the individual. An ad that is a 1.7 to one person may be a 0.9 to the next. Marketwide, impact quotient can only be approximated.

3. And, of course, the individual PEF is also unique; you may exceed one customer's expectations by 90 percent, then fall miserably short with the next. PEF can only be approximated marketwide.

So don't get all "left brain" about this stuff, okay? You can't measure it accurately. The only important thing is to be generally aware of the interaction between these factors.

Silva's CPE

My friend Jon Silva offers in-house financing on much of what he sells. The term in the credit industry for what Jon does is that he "carries his own paper," meaning that Jon actually loans his own money to his customers. Jon has become rich because Jon is a genius. When I asked him, "What rules do you use for determining who gets credit and how much credit they get?" Jon answered, "Rules are for fools. When the day is done, there are only 5 things that really matter: (1) the size of the down payment, (2) the amount of gross profit on the sale, (3) the credit history of the applicant, (4) the length of the loan's payout, and (5) the interest rate. You can let the customer have his own way with any one of the five as long as you control the other four. If I have a nice profit in the sale and the customer has a clean credit history, he can have anything in my store for nothing down, get a super-low interest rate, and take as long as he wants to pay it off. But if the profit is short or if the customer's credit history is weak, then it changes the whole equation. But give me a large enough profit in the sale, a big enough down payment, a short enough term, and a tall enough interest rate, and I'll carry paper on anyone."

It seems that Jon Silva has found his own "Credit Performance Equation." Now, if we could just bottle it, I'll bet we could sell it for a billion dollars.

39

A Coiled Cobra Called "Statistics"

classical mathematician will say, "Numbers don't lie," but a theoretical physicist will argue that they do. Me? I just say, "Figures lie when liars figure. You've got to be very careful with numbers."

Statistically, a flipped coin will land heads 50 percent of the time. But this fact is easily "proven" false by any contentious knothead with a quarter in his pocket. "I just flipped this quarter twice, and it came up heads both times." If the knothead is feeling generous, he can flip it twice more and announce, "Three heads, one tail, you're still wrong." After ten flips, "Seven heads and three tails. I have now proven beyond all doubt that your 50 percent theory is a load of bunk, pal." I bring up this knothead only to illustrate the dangers of being too narrow and specific in your interpretation of "mathematical fact." The fellow with a quarter "proved" only that he was a small-minded weasel when he failed to recognize that statistical properties emerge only on large scales.

See ch. 23, "Same Whiteboard, Same Trainer. . . ."

But there is equal danger in being too general in interpreting data. I refer specifically to the statistician who drowned while trying to wade across a river with an average depth of four feet. . . .

Day after day, media sales reps wage war with ad agency media buyers over the numbers published in ratings books. My newest employee in market research recently asked whether he should look at audience numbers only from the most recent ratings period or use a four-book average. "That depends," I said.

"It depends on what, exactly?"

I said, "Let's say a station had a 6 share in the spring book, an 8 share in summer, 10 in the fall, and 12 in the winter book. A four-book average would give this station a 9 share, but the 12 share in the most recent book is probably closer to the truth since its numbers have steadily been increasing. Go ahead and let that rep pitch you figures from the most recent book only."

I then reversed all the numbers on the white board to show a station with a 12 share in the spring book steadily declining to only a 6 share in the most recent book. Pointing at the new graph, I said, "This sales rep is the slippery weasel who's going to try to pitch you a four-book average. The truth is he's got a 6 share, but a four-book average would show him with a 9."

He asked, "So why don't we just always use the most recent ratings book?"

I then changed the numbers to show a station with an 11 share in the spring, a 12 share in the summer, another 12 share in the fall, and then a 7 share in the most recent ratings book. "There is such a thing as statistical error through faulty sampling," I said. "If upon investigation you find no reason for the sudden drop in this station's numbers, go ahead and allow the sales rep to make his presentation using a four-book average."

What should the rule be for ad agency media buyers? "Look for the Truth." And the rule for media sales reps? "Help them find it." I'm convinced that media buyers will become more open and approachable on the day that sales reps become more honest and forthright with the facts.

Or is that too much to ask?

The devil and his friend were walking down the street when they saw a man stoop down and pick up something from the ground, look at it, then put it in his pocket. The friend asked the devil, "What did that man pick up?" "He picked up a piece of Truth," said the devil. "That is a very bad business for you, then," said his friend. "Oh, not at all," the devil replied. "I'm going to help him organize it."

Hot Tip

The only time a ratings computer will lie to you is if you ask it to calculate a reach-and-frequency analysis based on a broad scheduling window. Example: Assume that a radio station has an average of 100,000 listeners at any moment between 6 AM and 9 AM, 80,000 listeners from 9 AM to 3 PM, 90,000 listeners from 3 PM to 7 PM, and 30,000 listeners from 7 PM to midnight. Ask the ratings computer to calculate a reach-and-frequency analysis for eighteen commercials per week, 6 AM to midnight, and the computer will assume that the eighteen ads are going to rotate evenly — in other words, that one of the ads will air from 6 AM to 7 AM, another from 7 AM to 8 AM, and so on. Based on this false assumption, the computer will report that your schedule would reach an average of 71,667 people each time it aired. But the scheduling computer will place most of your ads between 7 PM and midnight, since that would be completely within the terms of your contract. You're not going to reach 71,667 people each time your ad airs; you're going to reach 30,000. The stronger ad times between 6 AM and 7 PM are owned by those advertisers whose schedules specify 6 AM to 7 PM.

Television audiences are vastly larger at night, 7 PM to 11 PM*, than during the day. Conversely, radio audiences are larger during the daytime, 6 AM to 7 PM, than at night (though the audience swing is not nearly so radical as in television). Consequently, you should never agree to a scheduling window on television or radio that crosses the 7 PM hour. In other words, 6 AM to 7 PM is okay. 7 PM to midnight is okay. 3 PM to 10 PM is *not* okay in TV or in radio.

Please understand that I'm not saying, "Don't buy off-prime schedules." I'm saying only that you should never assume your ad is going to run at any time other than the worst time allowable by contract. Although my firm has a number of late-night and overnight radio schedules in cities coast to coast, we never schedule the ads as 24-hour rotators or calculate reach and frequency based on any scheduling window that crosses 7 PM.

To say it as plainly as possible: Never buy a broad rotator on television or radio, no matter how cheap the price.

The majority of media sales reps would prefer that you not know the things in this book. But if you're dealing with a media person who suggested that you read this book, or better yet, who bought it for you as a gift, then you're probably dealing with an honest person who is going to do his or her best to help you grow your business. ᴄᴥ

* In cities where the TV late-evening news airs at 10 PM, radio primetime is generally 6 AM–7 PM and TV prime is 7 PM–11 PM. But if the late-evening news is at 11 PM, then radio prime is generally 6 AM–8 PM and TV prime is 8 PM–midnight. Typically, the evening news is at 11 PM on both coasts and at 10 PM in the middle of America. Go figure.

40

How to Facilitate Brainstorming

Extraverts invented brainstorming. Stimulated by things external to them, extraverts "talk to think." But more than half of our population are introverted. Although equally as brilliant as extraverts, introverts "think to talk" and will rarely tell you what they are thinking, preferring to tell you only what they have already thought about. Consequently, introverts typically sit quietly through brainstorming sessions as they gather information to be processed later, when they have some time alone.

What a waste.

To have an awesome brainstorming session, just send everyone a detailed note twenty-four hours ahead of time that explains the issues to be discussed in tomorrow's brainstorming session. Extraverts will see the note only as an invitation and likely won't give it a second thought before the meeting. Introverts will interpret the note as a work assignment and begin formulating their thoughts on the subject to be discussed. Twenty-four hours later, having had a day to process and organize their thoughts, the introverts will immediately amaze you with the quality of their input. Stimulated by the discussion that has been launched by the introverts, the extraverts will also perform at a higher level than normal.

When you understand preferences, everybody wins. ❧

See ch. 26, "Getting to Know Yourself."

"Not everything we are capable of knowing and doing is accessible to or expressible in language. This means that some of our personal knowledge is off limits even to our own inner thoughts! Perhaps this is why humans are so often at odds with themselves, because there is more going on in our minds than we can ever consciously know."

— Dr. Richard E. Cytowic, neurologist

41

What We Say vs. What We Do

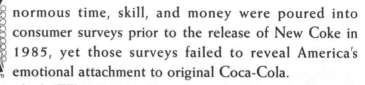

normous time, skill, and money were poured into consumer surveys prior to the release of New Coke in 1985, yet those surveys failed to reveal America's emotional attachment to original Coca-Cola.

When asked, "What is your favorite drink?" most people said, "Coke!" But when asked, "What do you have at home in your pantry right now?" their responses were quite different. Some people said Coke, some said Pepsi. Others said that they bought whatever was on sale, often a generic cola.

In 1983, Roy Stout, head of market research for Coca-Cola USA, said, "If we have twice as many vending machines, dominate fountain service, have more shelf space, spend more on advertising, and are competitively priced, why are we losing market share? You look at the Pepsi Challenge, and you have to begin asking about taste." Brian Dyson, president of Coca-Cola USA, agreed: "Maybe the way we assuage our thirst has changed. The characteristics that made Coke distinctive, like its bite, consumers now describe as harsh." Extensive research was launched, and a new, improved formula was ordered.

But long before we bought our first can, America had already decided that it hated New Coke, even though it was the flavor we had chosen in tens of thousands of taste tests. The surveyors asked us, "Which cola would you buy?" and we overwhelmingly picked the flavor that was New Coke. But a beverage is more than its flavor; a beverage is its marketing. And Coca-Cola had spent ninety-nine years convincing us that Coke was "the real thing," an integral part of American life, the red and white threads in the fabric of America.

When surveyed, most people will tell you what they honestly believe they would do if given the choice. Rarely, though, is this what they actually will do when faced with that choice.

There remains a persistent belief that the whole New Coke fiasco was merely a marketing ploy to remind us of how much we loved old Coke, but a close investigation of the facts clearly reveals otherwise. The simple truth is that a left-brain survey was conducted and a left-brain decision was made as a result of it.

New Coke is the kind of answer you get when you think with only half your brain.

See ch. 6, "Left, Right, Left, Right, Left, Right."

Some cynics will say that we planned the whole thing. . . . The truth is that we are not that smart.

Donald Keough, president of Coca-Cola in 1986,
when Classic Coke was reintroduced

42

Hmm...

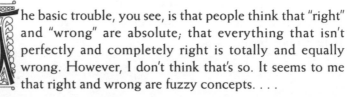he basic trouble, you see, is that people think that "right" and "wrong" are absolute; that everything that isn't perfectly and completely right is totally and equally wrong. However, I don't think that's so. It seems to me that right and wrong are fuzzy concepts. . . .

We get the notion that "right" and "wrong" are absolutes in the early grades, when children who know very little are taught by teachers who know very little more. Young children learn spelling and arithmetic, for instance, and here we tumble into apparent absolutes.

How do you spell "sugar"? Answer: s-u-g-a-r. That is right. Anything else is wrong.

Having exact answers, and having absolute rights and wrongs, minimizes the necessity of thinking, and that pleases both students and teachers. For that reason, students and teachers alike prefer short-answer tests to essay tests; multiple-choice over blank short-answer tests; and true-false tests over multiple choice.

But short-answer tests are, to my way of thinking, useless as a measure of a student's understanding of a subject. They are merely a test of the efficiency of his ability to memorize.

How do you spell "sugar"? Suppose Alice spells it p-q-z-z-f and Genevieve spells it s-h-u-g-e-r. Both are wrong, but is there any doubt that Alice is wronger than Genevieve?

Or suppose you spell "sugar" s-u-c-r-o-s-e, or C_{12}-H_{22}-O_{11}. Strictly speaking, you are wrong each time, but you're displaying a certain knowledge of the subject beyond conventional spelling.

Suppose then the test question was, "How many different ways can you spell 'sugar'? Justify each."

Naturally, the student would have to do a lot of thinking and, in the end, exhibit how much or how little he knows. The teacher would also have to do a lot of thinking in the attempt to evaluate how much or how little the student knows. Both, I imagine, would be outraged.

— Isaac Asimov, *The Relativity of Wrong*

"But that's spelling," you might object. "Were the question mathematical instead of grammatical, there could be only one correct answer." I imagine Asimov's reply: "Oh, really? Give me an example of such a question." You ask, "How much is 2 plus 2?" He quickly answers, "11," then adds, "to the base 3, of course." Seeing the loophole, you ask, "How much is 9 plus 5?" Looking at his watch, he answers, "5 hours past 9 would make it 2." Uh-oh — another loophole. Last chance. "Okay, then, how much is 9 plus 75?" Still looking at his watch, he answers immediately, "75 minutes past 9 would make it 10:15." He looks up at you. "Or would you like the answer in longitude?"

See ch. 2, "Perceptual Realities."

To better understand what just happened, we turn to Dr. Neil Postman, chair of the Department of Culture and Communications at New York University:

A question, even of the simplest kind, is not, and never can be, unbiased. The structure of any question is as devoid of neutrality as its content. The form of a question may ease our way or pose obstacles. Or, when even slightly altered, it may generate antithetical answers, as in the case of the two priests who, being unsure if it was permissible to smoke and pray at the same time, wrote to the Pope for a definitive answer. One priest phrased the question "Is it permissible to smoke while praying?" and was told it is not, since prayer should be the focus of one's whole attention; the other priest asked if it is permissible to pray while smoking and was told that it is, since it is always permissible to pray.

Now what was it again that you were saying about "objective" surveys? ଔ

43

BrandingBrandingBranding

People say the word "branding" as though it's a mysterious and complex proposition. But when you peel off all the layers of hype, it comes down to this: if advertising is "getting your name out," then branding is simply "attaching something to your name." A brand is the sum total of all the mental associations, good and bad, that are triggered by a name. What does your name stand for in the mind of the public? What are the mental associations triggered by "(fill in your name here)"?

Q: You mean it actually matters what I say in my ads?

A: Yeah. It actually matters.

Q: But I was led to believe that all I had to do was "reach the right people with my message."

A: And you believed it?

Demographic and psychographic targeting do have their place in strategic ad planning, but their importance has long been overrated. The painful crash of the NASDAQ in 2000 was due to the fact that America's dotcoms were reporting revenues far below projected levels and their burn rate of investor cash was being accelerated as a result. Investors in the Internet got out faster than a fat kid in dodgeball.

See ch. 16, "The Neurology of Branding."

Most Internet business plans called for enormous revenues to be generated through the sale of advertising. The Internet promised advertisers "ads precision-targeted to audience profiles," and "a stronger advertising solution that will better enable you to reach the right user at the right time." In *USA Today*'s tech report of November 5, 1999, Center for Media Education Executive Director Jeffrey Chester reported that "Internet ad networks do essentially all of their data gathering surreptitiously through 'cookies' placed on users' browsers.

Marketing databases, thanks to the Internet, now contain more information about consumers' purchasing habits than ever before."

But a short eight months later, on July 17, 2000, the *Potomac Tech Journal's* Steve Robblee reported "growing evidence that Web advertisers are dissatisfied. . . . More than 9 in 10 Web-based businesses are not happy with the results of paid banner ads." In response to this, Advertising.com promised that its new goal would be "to better target advertising messages to the right demographic groups."

Huh?

Even though it may seem counterintuitive, the simple truth is that the advertiser's message, itself, is far more important than the vehicle of its delivery. Successful branding depends on your ability to speak to the customer in the language of the customer about what matters to the customer. The goal of branding is simply to be the name that customers think of immediately whenever they, or anyone they know, need what you sell. Branding is about the message.

The analytical sales reps of the Internet preached that "psychographic targeting" was all that really mattered. They were tragically mistaken. Their ads failed miserably, and the sales reps who promised miracles through "targeting" are now mostly unemployed.

You haven't built your branding campaign around "reaching the right people" and forgotten about the importance of associative ad copy, have you? ❧

44

Frosting

Named after the poet Robert Frost, "Frosting" is the simplest and gentlest technique for transforming drab communication into razor-edged wordsmanship.

The essence of Frosting is to replace common, predictable phrases with unexpected, interesting ones. The goal is simply to surprise Broca with elegant combinations of words.

To better understand Frosting, we'll de-Frost Robert Frost's powerful poem "Misgiving." Compare the language in the de-Frosted poem below with the corresponding phrases in the original, fully Frosted version that follows it.

See ch. 19, "The Tollbooth on the Yellow Brick Road."

The leaves all shouted, "We will go with you, O wind!"
They said they would follow him to the end.
But they got sleepy as they went along,
So they tried to convince him to stay with them.

Ever since they got started way back last spring
The leaves had been looking forward to this flight,
But now they would rather hide behind a wall
Or lie under some bushes to spend the night.

And now when the wind yells at them to come along,
They answer him with less and less vigor.
At most they just move around a little,
But they don't move very fast. Go figure.

I'd like to believe that when I am dead,
And can finally find out what there is to it,
And learn all the mysteries beyond the grave
That I won't be like them . . . too tired to do it.

104

De-Frosted, the story has the feel of those tacky little third-grade limericks, doesn't it?

Now let's read the poem as Frost originally wrote it. Take note of the vivid, concise mental images created through Frost's unusual combinations of common words, and how he plunges you quickly into the action with an early verb.

Exercise: Find a few paragraphs you've written, and without changing the message structurally, replace all the common predictable phrases with unexpected, interesting ones. Whip a little Frosting on it.

All crying, "We will go with you, O Wind!"
The foliage follow him, leaf and stem;
But a sleep oppresses them as they go,
And they end by bidding him stay with them.

Since ever they flung abroad in spring
The leaves had promised themselves this flight,
Who now would fain seek sheltering wall,
Or thicket, or hollow place for the night.

And now they answer his summoning blast
With an ever vaguer and vaguer stir,
Or at utmost a little reluctant whirl
That drops them no further than where they were.

I only hope that when I am free
As they are free to go in quest
Of the knowledge beyond the bounds of life
It may not seem better to me to rest.

An interesting metaphor for death, don't you think?

What associations are carried by the word "quest"?

105

45

Seussing

LIFE magazine, April 6, 1959: "If you should ask [Dr. Seuss] how he ever thought up an animal called a Bippo-no-Bungus from the wilds of Hippo-no-Hungus or a Tizzle-Topped Tufted Mazurka from the African island of Yerka, his answer would be disarmingly to the point: 'Why, I've been to most of those places myself, so the names are from memory. As for the animals, I have a special dictionary which gives most of them, and I just look up their spellings.'"

The technique I call "Seussing" is simply making up your own new words. Do you have the courage to do it? Nothing delights Broca quite so much as instinctively knowing the meaning of a word that he's never before heard. Sitting in the tollbooth of the brain, the ever-watchful Broca hates predictability, but he's always delighted by the elegant unexpected.

Dr. Seuss understood the danger of predictability. While each of his stories had a moral, he was careful never to start with one. "Kids," he said, "can see a moral coming a mile off and they gag at it." Therefore Dr. Seuss allowed each story's moral to develop on its own. Never was it forced or contrived. When a writer is surprised by the ending of his own story, and by the moral message it contains, you can bet the reader will be, too.

Another function of Broca's area of the brain is to attach imagined actions to the words you and I call verbs. Since Broca guards the door leading into the imagination, it only stands to reason that verbs are more important to persuasion than nouns, words that are attached to persons, places, and things in Wernicke's area at the other end of the brain. Seuss somehow knew this intuitively. In *Pipers at the Gates of Dawn*, Jonathan Cott describes meeting a seventy-six-year-old Dr. Seuss in

WizardSwords

Seussing: making up new words that express an idea by virtue of their sound, tone, context, and associations.

See ch. 19, "The Tollbooth on the Yellow Brick Road."

July 1980 and discussing with him the work of Kornei Chukovsky, a Russian children's poet who in 1925 wrote a book about how to win and hold their attention. One of Chukovsky's strongest suggestions in the book was to "avoid using too many adjectives and, instead, to use more verbs." Seuss emphatically agreed.

Likewise, the good doctor understood that to win the voluntary attention of young children (the world's most inattentive audience) he would need to enter the realm of the illogical, nonjudgmental right brain first, then proceed to the rational, logical left. Dr. Seuss books proceed from the simple premise that children will believe a ludicrous situation if it is pursued with relentless logic. "If I start with a two-headed animal," Seuss said, "I must never waver from that concept. There must be two hats in the closet, two toothbrushes in the bathroom, and two sets of spectacles on the night table. Then my readers will accept the poor fellow without hesitation and so will I."

Will you dive — splash! — into the right brain before swimming over to the left? Are you paying close attention to your verbs? Do you have the audacity to moon predictability by using a word that's not official? Seussing, like pepper sauce, is powerful. A tiny bit adds zip to even the blandest of dishes.

Seuss up your message; use a word they've never heard.

"When they read to me poems that have been taught to them in school . . . they have been taught hackneyed lines, absurd rhythms, cheap rhymes. There are times when I could cry with disappointment."

— Kornei Chukovsky

See ch. 21, "Below Deck in a Storm at Sea," and ch. 100+1, "Dr. Seuss on Writing for Children."

46

Being Monet

Blurry, bright, Impressionist paintings aren't about details or accuracy. In fact, Claude Monet said that he hoped "to capture the first impression of an image; that moment before the eye or camera focused." He said he was striving for "instantaneity."

In 1869, Monet was painting at La Grenouillère when he realized that shadows are not just black or brown but are influenced by their surrounding colors. He further realized that the

> **color** of an object is modified by the
>> **light** in which it is seen, by
>>> **reflections** from other objects, and by
>>>> **contrast** with juxtaposed colors.

Likewise, the meaning of a word is influenced by the surrounding words. The

> **color** of a word is modified by the
>> **light** (context) in which it is seen, by
>>> **reflections** from words near it, and by
>>>> **contrast** with words juxtaposed to it.

Monet considered black to be the total lack of color: "Though shadows are darker than surrounding colors, they still contain some degree of color. Therefore, shadows are not black." As a result, Monet virtually eliminated void, empty black from his palette of paints.

When Monet minimized his use of black, his remaining colors sprang to life.

> **Light** radiated from his canvas.
>> **Reflections** became luminous.
>>> **Contrasts**, magical.
>>>> **Images**, worth million$.

Likewise, to speak Monet, you must eliminate empty, void "black words" from your sentences. Light will radiate from the words remaining. Persuasion will become luminous. Results, magical. Refine this, and you will own a talent worth million$.

The fundamental principles of being Monet:

1. Ignore the details.
2. Exaggerate the color.
3. Remove the black.

It's not about making perfect sense. It's right-brain language, impressionistic and dazzling.

WizardSwords

Frosting: replacing common, predictable phrases with unexpected, interesting ones.

being Monet: speaking impressionistically, rather than precisely, by using poetic exaggeration and overstatement and selecting words according to the intensity of their associations, or "color." To speak in incomplete sentences due to the removal of "black words." Being Monet might be thought of as radical, accelerated Frosting.

instantaneity: engaging the imagination with a vivid and electric first mental image (FMI).

black words: words that do not contribute toward a more vivid and colorful mental image (but, and, that, therefore, etc.)

Daguerre: a derogatory term, used to describe a style of writing that is factual, tedious, and colorless. Most academic writing is "Daguerre."

I was born and grew up in Baltic marshland
by zinc-grey breakers that always marched on
in twos. Hence all rhymes, hence that wan flat voice
that ripples between them like hair still moist,
if it ripples at all. Propped on a pallid elbow,
the helix picks out of them no sea rumble
but a clap of canvas, of shutters, of hands, a kettle
on the burner, boiling — Lastly, the seagull's metal cry.

Opening lines of "A Part of Speech"
Joseph Brodsky
Poet Laureate of the United States, 1992–1996

47

Power Monet

Perhaps the definitive writer of "Monet" in our generation is the great Paul Simon. To all who would follow him into the electric wonderland of literary Impressionism, he offers this advice:

If you want to write a song about the moon, walk along the craters of the afternoon when the shadows are deep and the light is alien and gravity leaps like a knife off the pavement. If you want to write a song about the heart, think about the moon before you start, because the heart will howl like a dog in the moonlight and the heart can explode like a pistol on a June night. So if you want to write a song about the heart and its ever-longing for a counterpart, write a song about the moon.

Hey, songwriter, if you want to write a song about a face, think about a photograph that you really can't remember . . . but can't erase. Wash your hands in dreams and lightning. Cut off your hair, and whatever is frightening, if you want to write a song about a face. If you want to write a song about the human race, write a song about the moon. If you want to write a song about the moon . . . if you want to write a spiritual tune . . . then do it. . . . Write a song about the moon.

> — Paul Simon's advice to writers
> in "Song about the Moon"
> from his album *Hearts and Bones*
> © 1981, Warner Bros. Records

You should go buy this CD if you don't already own it. ❧

48

Sneak Past the Security Guard

Doubt is what happens when the security guard of the rational, logical left brain isn't sure whether to accept an idea or not. But unlike his left-brain counterpart, the right brain doesn't make judgments at all. He isn't concerned in the least about plausibility; that's the left brain's job. So when your idea is rejected at the door of the left brain, just knock on Righty's door. He'll let anyone in. Once inside the mind, your idea can scoot over to the logical left on the waterslide of symbolic thought.

There are several ways this can be done. One of them is to use an anapest: "For the moon never beams/without bringing me dreams/ of the beautiful Annabel Lee."* An anapest is a rhythmic pattern of syllables composed of two light stresses followed by a heavy third stress. (Anapests don't have to rhyme, but often do.) Since anapests are inherently musical, they enter directly into the nonjudgmental right brain, and upon crossing over to the left (via the dorsolateral prefrontal association area) they often become stuck in the phonological loop.

In other words, you can't get them out of your head. Ever notice how much easier it is to recall phrases that have a lyrical beat?

Relentlessly subjected to a constant barrage of advertising, the average person today feels like a juror in the O. J. Simpson trial with 900 exhibits, 433 motions, and 126 witnesses providing an overwhelming glut of tedious data, facts, and figures. In the end, most legal analysts agree that O. J.'s "not guilty" verdict swung on Johnnie Cochran's relentless serenade to the jurors: "If it doesn't fit, you must acquit."

In the jury deliberation room, as the twelve tried to fit all the data into a clear, coherent picture, Cochran's anapest echoed in their

* In this anapest by Edgar Allan Poe, the words "for" and "the" are light stresses, and the word "moon" is a heavy stress; this is the first anapestic unit. "Never" has two syllables, both light stresses, then "beams" is heavy, the second anapestic unit. "Without" has two syllables, both light, then "bring" is heavy stress — thus, anapestic unit number three; "-ing" and "me" are light, then "dreams" is heavy, the fourth anapestic unit, etc.

I strongly agree with the good doctor. The message is the message. There are many techniques for strengthening a good message, but you can never really compensate for a message that has no relevance. In this chapter you were given a few simple techniques for making a good message better, but techniques are not gimmicks. Frankly, I don't like gimmicks, and I'm not often drawn to people who do. You can never satisfy a gimmickmonger.

See ch. 19, "The Tollbooth on the Yellow Brick Road."

brains. Cochran further assured them repeatedly that "Simpson could not, would not, did not commit these crimes." Had Cochran presented a rational, logical, left-brain definition of "reasonable doubt" to the jurors, O. J. would probably not be walking the streets today.

Where did Johnnie Cochran learn about the magic of the anapest? Most likely, it was at his mother's knee. "Oh, the sea is so full of a number of fish, if a fellow is patient, he might get his wish! And that's why I think that I'm not such a fool when I sit here and fish in McElligot's Pool!" Yes, it was in 1937 that the good Dr. Seuss began using anapestic meter almost exclusively.

Alcohol is absorbed directly into the blood through the lining of the stomach, completely bypassing the body's digestive system; that's what makes it dangerous. Employing a rhythm, particularly an anapest, is like serving alcohol to a listener. But it's just one of the ways that you can sneak a message past Broca, the uptight little security guard of the mind. The other three ways are humor, mental participation, and subliminal associations.

1. Humor enters the left brain, then surprises Broca with a punch line that he "didn't see coming." Bingo, you're in.

2. Mental participation, or drama, begins in the dorsolateral prefrontal association area between Broca's area and the prefrontal cortex, then crosses over into the right brain as the listener/reader/viewer begins imagining experiences she's never had. But if the left-brain security guard is on high alert, he'll notice what you're trying to do and will become as cautious as a long-tailed cat in a room full of rocking chairs. But don't worry. There's still a window that you can crawl through, and it's never guarded. I'm talking about:

3. Subliminal associations. When California's conservatives wanted to define the word "marriage" by law, Proposition 22 was added to the California ballot. It was officially titled the "Defense of Marriage Act." As the date for voting drew near, it became apparent that the proposition was going to lose by a wide margin. Finally, a wizard said, "The meaning of a word is always bigger than its definition; words carry associations. The word 'defense' is a violent word, conjuring associative memories of 'national defense' and 'defense budget.' It makes us think of Vietnam and bloodshed. And what is the 'marriage act'? Sex. Juxtapose the word 'Defense' with 'Marriage Act' and you get a very uncomfortable feeling. The subconscious image is that of a battered wife, defending herself in a marriage, or of a woman defending herself from sexual assault. No one wants to vote for a thing called the Defense of Marriage Act."

With just a few weeks to go, the new ads began talking about "Proposition 22, the Protection of Marriage Act."

It won by a landslide. "Protect" and "Defend" may mean the same thing in a dictionary, but they're radically different in the human mind.

On high alert, Broca can anticipate and defend against any attempt at subversion through humor or mental participation, but poetic meter is a bit more subtle. Most subtle of all, however, are subliminal associations, since they're not introduced from outside the listener, but arise within the listener's own mind.

Standing on shore, looking out to sea, who can stop the rising of the tide?

Oh, yes, words are a powerful force. ❧

49

Lists, Steps, and Rules

hen Stephen Covey listed the seven habits of those who are left-brain dominant, did he mean to imply that we who prefer the romance of the right brain cannot be "highly effective people"? Sadly, most of America lives within the confines of a narrow mental universe defined by the left-brainers. We are in the thrall of enumerators — people who are constantly compiling lists of the top 500 companies, the top 100 places to live, the top 10 TV shows, and so on and so on. This is a very left-brain way of trying to understand what's going on, but it provides only a narrow, linear sense of reality.

Nevertheless, we let this compulsive numbering of things tell us how to live our lives. To gain a sense of control, however illusory, we search endlessly for numbered lists. A plethora of books have been written for those who prefer the clarity of steps and rules to the ambiguity of guiding principles. These books usually sell very well:

The 100 Absolutely Unbreakable Laws of Business Success, by Brian Tracy

The 55 Steps to Outrageous Service, by Greg Hatcher

The 48 Laws of Power, by Robert Greene

The 22 Immutable Laws of Branding, by Laura Ries

The 21 Irrefutable Laws of Leadership, by John C. Maxwell

The 12 Gateways to Personal Growth, by Dan Millman

The 11 Immutable Laws of Internet Branding, by Al Ries

The 10 Natural Laws of Successful Time and Life Management, by Hyrum W. Smith

The 9 Natural Laws of Leadership, by Warren Blank (Didn't Maxwell just say there were 21?)

The 9 Steps to Financial Freedom, by Suze Orman

The 7 Spiritual Laws of Success, by Deepak Chopra

The 7 Habits of Highly Effective People, by Stephen Covey

The 7 Steps to Passionate Love, by William Van Horn

The 6 Steps to Songwriting Success, by Jason Blume

The 5 Steps to Successful Selling, by Zig Ziglar

The 4 Laws of Debt Free Prosperity, by Blaine Harris

The 3 Steps to Yes, by Gene Bedell

Did you notice that no one ever publishes a list of 8? This is most likely because people who come up with 8 things either drop one or add one. Eight just doesn't "feel" right; the associations just aren't as good as with 7 or 9. Why? Perhaps because "8" is a homonym for "ate" and brings to mind "hate," whereas "7" rhymes with "heaven" and is everybody's lucky number. Nine? That's how many months we spend in the womb, the most peaceful time of our life.

Once, in a moment of weakness, I myself listed the "Twelve Causes of Advertising Failure" (*The Wizard of Ads,* chapter 35). I might just as easily have named 17, 61, or 183 causes, but I chose 12 because it's a number of completeness and gives the reader more confidence in the authority of the list. There are 12 months in a year, 12 hours on a clock face, 12 signs of the Zodiac. Twelve is useful because it's evenly divisible by a lot of numbers: 2, 3, 4, and 6. Are you beginning to understand why recovery groups typically embrace a 12-step program?

Numbers, words, colors, and names all carry mental associations. Can I say "365" without your thinking, "days in a year"? Your ability to "brand" is determined by your understanding of the associative images that will be conjured by the numbers, words, colors, names, shapes, and pictures that you present to the customer.

An ad always says more than it says. What do your ads say? ॐ

50
Frameline Magnetism

Muskogee, Oklahoma, 1965, Hilldale Elementary School, Mrs. Shelton's second-grade class: One by one, we march to the front of the room to recite the poems we've written. It's Reggie Gibson's turn. "Spider, Spider, on the wall. Ain't you got no smarts at all? Don't you know that wall's fresh plastered? Get off that wall, you dirty . . . (long pause) spider." The class explodes. Mrs. Shelton is not amused. Reggie Gibson has discovered frameline magnetism.

The edge of a picture is called the frameline. When an image extends beyond the frameline, the viewer's imagination reacts by filling in what was left outside the frame. This phenomenon is called frameline magnetism, and it's a powerful tool that has long been used by the world's great photographers, videographers, filmmakers, and illustrators to engage the imagination of a viewer.

The first time I ever used verbal frameline magnetism was in an ad for my first client, Woody Justice. I had written almost verbatim what Woody had said to me on the phone in a moment of frustration. Then, looking at what I was holding, I saw the core of a powerful radio script that would become a true pouring-out of Woody's heart to the public. I didn't want to shatter the intimate moment by jamming the store's address and phone number into the ad, so I persuaded Woody to let me leave them out. At the end of the ad, when listeners were expecting the predictable blah, blah, blah of a store address and phone number, they heard only a moment's pregnant pause, then Woody saying off-mike: "Okay, I'm done." And that was all.

Radio listeners were stunned by what wasn't there. Although it's been well over a decade, people in Missouri still talk about that ad.

That which is not spoken often speaks the loudest. ꙮ

Numerous examples of frameline magnetism, both in photography and in words, can be seen in the companion book to *Magical Worlds.* Available in bookstores and from most online sellers, it's titled *Accidental Magic: The Wizard's Techniques for Writing Words Worth 1,000 Pictures.*

"Talk low, talk slow, and don't say too much."
— John Wayne's advice to actors

51
Being Perfectly (Robert) Frank

Robert Frank is generally regarded as one of the greatest photographers the world has ever seen. In his legendary photo book, *The Americans,* Frank captures the unposed reality of 1955–56 America with such ruthless clarity that collectors now bid tens of thousands of dollars to own just one of his vintage prints.

At the drive-in theater, Robert Frank would be in the car behind you, aiming his camera through the windshield to capture what it felt like to be at a drive-in movie at sundown. At the political rally, Frank wasn't interested in the practiced smile of the up-and-coming politician, but would take his photos from behind the man in such a way that made you feel the pressure that was on the candidate and sense the energy in the air. At the opera on opening night, when all the other photographers were crowded into "the one, good spot to shoot from," Robert Frank would be down in the orchestra pit, letting you see what the conductor was seeing and making you feel what the conductor was feeling.

Robert Frank was (1) unusual in his selection of an angle, (2) economical in his inclusion of detail, and (3) a master of frameline magnetism. Isn't it interesting that these are precisely the same three techniques that Ernest Hemingway used to become one of the most respected novelists in history?

Speaking of the unusual angle, or perspective, from which he typically approached a story, Hemingway once said, "In stating as fully as I could how things really were, it was often very difficult and I wrote awkwardly and the awkwardness is what they called my style. All mistakes and awkwardness are easy to see, and they called it style."

Poor Faulkner. Does he really think big emotions come from big words? He thinks I don't know the ten-dollar words. I know them all right. But there are older and simpler and better words, and those are the ones I use.

— Ernest Hemingway

In his photographs, Robert Frank excluded all but the barest and most necessary elements. Likewise, Hemingway's writing style was economical, using simple words to create detached, impersonal descriptions of action that captured the scene precisely. Simple details in black and white, no romantic exaggeration. Like Frank, Hemingway was deeply concerned with authenticity. His goal was to provide readers with the raw material of an actual experience.

Here's how Hemingway described frameline magnetism: "I always try to write on the principle of the iceberg. There is seven-eighths of it under water for every part that shows. Anything you know you can eliminate and it only strengthens your iceberg. It is the part that doesn't show."

WizardSwords

Robert Frank: a style of writing that is accurate, but very selective in its inclusion of detail, and that approaches the subject from an unusual angle.

putting it underwater: editing or deleting information under the assumption that it is already known to the listener.

Principles of Being Perfectly (Robert) Frank

1. Choose a revealing angle. Put the reader/listener/viewer on the scene.

2. Select your details sparingly. Include only what's interesting. And barely that.

3. Put the known "under water." Never tell the reader/listener/viewer anything he already knows or can figure out for himself.

To write Robert Frank is to communicate in the fewest words and from the most interesting perspective. It's how to speak to the left brain with accuracy and clarity without being boring.

52

A Higher Level of Order

You hope to attract and hold the attention of another. Your goal is to fascinate that person's mind. You are a teacher, a minister, a romantic suitor, or possibly an advertiser. Is there a successful model for attracting and holding human attention that you can study? Indeed there is.

Humans are attracted by ocean waves, clouds, mountains, lightning, and logs burning in the fireplace, and we think snowflakes are beautiful. We detect an elegant order in each of these that our minds cannot fully grasp. This marvelous order is known to science as chaos, and it is beyond the ability of the mind to predict. (Predictability, you will recall, is the mortal enemy of persuasion, because predictability triggers boredom. Remember Broca? Hmm. . . . this could be useful.)

Using business problem topology, let's begin by looking at the defining characteristics of chaotic systems:

1. Chaotic systems are deterministic; they have something determining their behavior.

2. Chaotic systems are very sensitive to their initial conditions. A very slight change in the starting point can lead to an enormously different outcome.

3. Chaotic systems may appear to be disorderly, even random, but they are not. Beneath the seemingly random behavior is a pattern of elegant order. Truly random systems are not chaotic.

If you consider that mapping a chaotic system can easily require tens of millions of notations, you can easily see why it was only after computers were invented that we were able to see these patterns. Until then, the patterns were too big to comprehend.

Using chaotic mathematical equations, computers today are producing images that look exactly like the beauty we see in nature. Amazingly, these chaotic maps also seem to mirror the behavior of the stock exchange and population fluctuations and chemical reactions. We call such chaotic maps "fractals." Examples of natural fractals are clouds, coastlines, lightning, and mountains.

Benoit Mandelbrot, a scientist at IBM, created additional fractal images by mapping the variations in stock market prices, the probabilities of words in English, and the motion of turbulent fluids, because each of these has a pattern that is slightly beyond our human ability to predict.

Are you now beginning to understand why people are drawn to

1. playing the stock market,

2. listening to the combination of rhythm and words in poetry and song, and

3. staring at the sea? ∾

Mandelbrot has since become a professor of mathematics at Harvard. In 1985, he was awarded the Barnard Medal for Meritorious Service to Science. The following year he received the Franklin Medal. Two years later he was honored with the Alexander von Humboldt Prize. He received the Steinmetz Medal in 1988 and later was honored with many more awards, including the Nevada Medal in 1991.

A fractal is the map of a chaotic system, composed of millions of points that seem, at first, to be random.

The truth always turns out to be simpler than you thought.

Richard Feynman

120

53

Glimpsing Chaos

A man driven by curiosity will often discover that he is riding on a train whose tracks he did not lay, one small part of a pattern bigger than he can see.

My train ride into chaos began with an odd bit of trivia. "For want of a nail, the shoe was lost. For want of a shoe, the horse was lost. For want of a horse, the rider was lost. For want of a rider, the battle was lost. For want of that battle, the kingdom was lost. . . . over a horseshoe nail."

Although this quote is routinely attributed to Benjamin Franklin's *Poor Richard's Almanack* of 1758, it was originally published in George Herbert's *Jacula Prudentum* of 1633. That tiny horseshoe nail of trivia sent me tumbling down the rabbit hole into Wonderland. (I said hello to Alice for you. She said to tell you Hi.) I stumbled upon this trivia while attempting to isolate the common denominator in hit songs. My hypothesis was simply this: If people from coast to coast simultaneously agree, "We like this song!" then there must be a basis for their agreement. I was trying to find that basis.

My method of investigation revolved around the "one-hit wonders" of the past forty years — specifically those artists who emerged out of nowhere to hit the top of the charts, never to be heard from again. I further narrowed my focus to include only those hits that stayed on the charts for a while and are still widely remembered. Finally, I chose only the hits recorded by people who continued to record new songs following their hit, but who were never able to break another one. I then compared the hit with all the other songs the same group recorded later. What did the hit song have that their other songs didn't?

I noticed a funny sort of mathematical recurrence that seemed to involve the number three. I mentioned this to my phenomenally well-read and highly respected psychologist friend, Dr. Nick Grant. He said, "Augustine of Hippo once saw threes all around him. You should read the book he wrote about it: *On the Trinity.* I think it was published in the year 410." (Smart guy, huh?)

I located *On the Trinity,* stumbled upon the second horseshoe nail, and met the Cheshire Cat in chapter 2 of book 15, when Augustine asks and answers his own question: "Why does it say in the holy Psalm that the hearts of them shall rejoice that seek the Lord, that seek His face forever? Why does it not say that the hearts of them shall rejoice that find the Lord? If that which is always being sought seems as though it will never be found, how then will the hearts of them that seek rejoice, and not rather be made sad, if they cannot find what they seek? For the holy Psalm does NOT say, The hearts shall rejoice of them that find, but of them that seek, the Lord." Augustine then speculates that joy must be born "when one has been able to find how incomprehensible that is which he was seeking." In other words, Augustine hypothesized that we are drawn toward that which is beyond our comprehension. The joy is in the seeking . . . in the attempt to grasp . . . in the stretching to make room in the mind.

While researching one-hit wonders and the number three, I was also investigating the science of topology so that I might better understand how best to use it to discover business innovation models. In my studies I learned that the originator of topology, Henri Poincaré, also gave us the modern qualitative theory of dynamical systems. He created topology, the study of shapes and their continuity, only to use as a mathematical tool in his attempt to answer the question "Is the solar system stable?" It seems that King Oscar II of Sweden had offered a large cash prize to whoever could answer the question definitively. Poincaré won the prize with his publication of *On the Problem of Three Bodies and the Equations of Equilibrium.* In his attempt to solve the problem, Poincaré introduced the Poincaré section and saw the first signs of chaos.

I'll not attempt to explain, at this time, the psychological phenomena of divergence, convergence, compression, and transition that I discovered as a result of studying Poincaré's work. Suffice it to say that they are the universal signatures of every hit song, television show, movie, and best-selling novel in history. ⌘

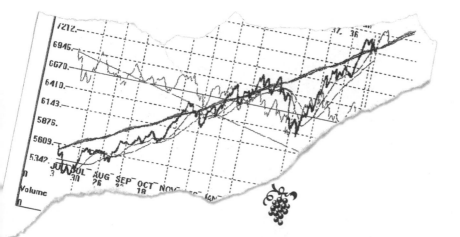

A child of five would understand this. Send someone to fetch a child of five.

Groucho Marx

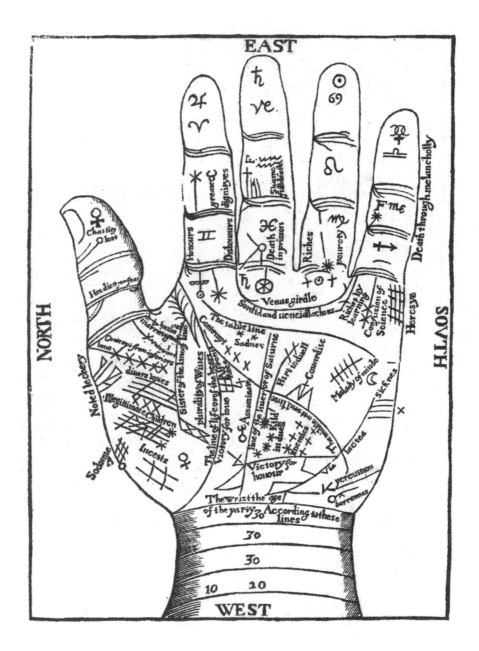

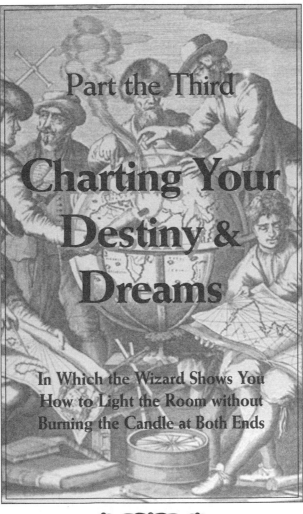

Part the Third

Charting Your Destiny & Dreams

In Which the Wizard Shows You
How to Light the Room without
Burning the Candle at Both Ends

54

The Beagle in Your Brain

beagle's nose has four times the volume of a lawyer's nose and more than 200 million ethmoidal (olfactory) cells, compared with only 5 million in the nose of the lawyer. The beagle has no understanding of the law, but in scientific tests has proven herself more than one million times more able to pick up the scent of a rabbit. Due to the fact that they're always running off, beagles are often thought to be stupid. Nothing could be further from the truth.

The beagle lives in your brain's right hemisphere, ever sniffing for important clues. Her name is "Intuition," and she's legendary for the wisdom of her nose. But the analytical lawyer in your logical left brain doesn't understand the beagle's wordless, right-brain logic; he thinks she's just wasting valuable time. The lawyer always has a purpose, a destination, an agenda, and a plan. With his watch on his wrist and his map in hand, the lawyer is leading the beagle through the Forest of Information when suddenly, "Aroooo! Aroooo! Aroooo!" the beagle takes off like a rocket. "Damn that beagle!" says the lawyer. "We don't have time for this!"

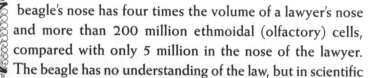

"Put your coat on."
"Why?"
"Because it's cold outside."
"Why?"
"Because it's wintertime."
"Why?"
"Because the Earth's axis is tilted 23.4° from perpendicular to its orbital plane."

WizardSwords

the Beagle: a hungry curiosity, hot on the trail of a discovery.

"Why?"

"You ask too many questions."

As a little kid, did you ever wonder what number, exactly, was "too many"? If you did, you quickly learned that "too many" wasn't a number at all, but a certain kind of question — the kind that people cannot easily answer. When you discovered that complex or impulsive questions annoyed the people around you, you quit asking those kinds of questions. Soon you abandoned complex and impulsive thoughts altogether.

Oh, what a sad, dark day when the lawyer leashed your beagle.

Has your life grown a bit stale and predictable? Would you like to have an adventure? Renew your childhood relationship with the beagle in your brain, then follow her as she follows her nose. Curiosity is the beagle's fuel; provide her with all you can muster. But be prepared — the wordless beagle Intuition lives in your right brain, where chaotic patterns thrive amidst its ten thousand billion synapses, so she knows of hidden trails and interconnected relationships that are far too vast to be seen on the tiny little view screen of your conscious comprehension. What may appear to you to be aimless wandering is actually the beagle's focused pursuit of a quarry.

Just as Jack traded his cow for three magic beans and the Magi presented their three gifts in Bethlehem, the Wizard now gives you three magical words of advice: "Free the beagle." There's no telling where your beagle will take you, but I'll wager that you'll be startled and delighted each time you find yourself in exactly the right place, at exactly the right time.

It's a magical world out there. Are you ready to go exploring?

127

55

What Are You All About?

Life is what happens to you while you're busy making other plans.

— John Lennon

Like messages in bottles, we ride the waves of circumstance. Tossed this way and that by unexpected developments, our secret hope is to be plucked from the ocean by a strong and purposeful hand. Discovered.

Human beings have a need to belong. We desire a purpose, a direction, a plan. But these are treasures that few drifting bottles can boast. Most of us simply go with the flow and have no answer when asked how we will measure success.

What will be your message to the world? What fingerprint will you leave on it when you're through? What is your "someday" goal? Do you have a North Star, a guiding hope that helps you choose the right way at each crossroads? Or have you fallen into the glassy-eyed stupor of living one day at a time?

Success cannot be measured in dollars. Neither can it be measured in health or longevity. To say that your goal is "happiness" is far too vague an answer. How will you measure success? How will you recognize it when it arrives?

You've always known that you can be and do whatever you really want. Sadly, few people know what they want. Do you?

Jack raises a forefinger and tells Billy that the secret of happiness is "one thing." In classic left-brain style, Billy spends the next three days trying to figure out what that "one thing" might be. Had Billy not been quite so linear and sequential, he might have realized that Jack was simply trying to tell him that, to be truly happy, he must give himself utterly and completely to "one thing" — something, anything.

To what are you committed? What is your "one thing"? You haven't been confusing transient, temporary pleasures with true and abiding happiness, have you?

Happiness will grow in no soil other than the soil of commitment. The root of happiness is loyalty, as only from loyalty can the stalk of self-image shoot skyward. Personal interests and accomplishments are merely the branches that reach out from the stalk of self-image. Joy, peace, and contentment are its leaves basking warmly in the sun.

Without the soil of commitment and the root of loyalty, there can be no leaves of joy, peace, and contentment.

To be truly happy, you've got to know who you are.

It is your loyalties and your commitments that define you. Likewise, it is from these loyalties and commitments that your dreams and goals emerge. (Tell me your recurrent daydreams and I'll tell you who you are.)

Sadder than living your whole life without ever achieving your dream would be to live your life without dreaming. But perhaps the greatest tragedy of all would be to have a dream and achieve it, never realizing that happiness is not the reward at the summit of the climb.

Happiness is the climb.

"For a long time it had seemed to me that life was about to begin — real life. But there was always some obstacle in the way, something to be gotten through first, some unfinished business, time still to be served, or a debt to be paid. Then life would begin. At last it dawned on me that these obstacles were my life."

— Alfred D'Souza

A man saw a ball of gold in the sky;
He climbed for it,
And eventually he achieved it —
It was clay.
Now this is the strange part:
When the man went to the earth
And looked again,
Lo, there was the ball of gold.
Now this is the strange part:
It was a ball of gold.
Aye, by the heavens, it was a ball of gold.

Stephen Crane (1871–1900)

56

Dreams and Contentment

I feel sorry for people who have never learned how to celebrate the ordinary; who live their lives under the sad illusion that happiness is just beyond their fingertips. "As soon as I find my soul mate . . . get out of debt . . . find a better job . . . then I'll be happy."

But I also pity the pale souls who carry no dream within them that is bigger than they are, those timid shadows who are unwilling to step into the light and boldly attempt the impossible. Last week a visitor to our building said, "Always expect the worst and you'll never be disappointed." I looked closely at him for a wry smile, a twinkle in his eyes, or some other signal that he was joking. He wasn't. I avoided him the rest of that day and then breathed a huge sigh of relief when he was finally gone.

Am I crazy? Is it wrong for me to feel sorry for those who think happiness lies just beyond their fingertips, while at the same time pitying those who fear to reach for things beyond their grasp?

I believe, unconditionally, that you should be content exactly as you are. But I also believe that you should reach for the stars. Although these beliefs, on the surface, appear to contradict one another, on another level they are perfectly compatible. In the words of the great physicist Niels Bohr, "The opposite of a correct statement is a false statement. The opposite of a profound truth may well be another profound truth."

Our universe is built on mutually exclusive truths.

Mutually exclusive truths will always contain at least one common ingredient. In this instance, that common ingredient is an absence of fear. Being content and reaching for the stars both require an absence of fear. The fear of being average robs you of contentment.

The fear of failure robs you of the joy of your dreams. Fear is an unrewarding master.

No one should live without goals and dreams and visions of grand possibilities, but you should never let them rob you of the ability to celebrate the ordinary. Colorful and happy dreams will bring joy into your life, regardless of whether or not you ever achieve them. Your dreams, loyalties, relationships, and faith form the essence of who you are.

And who you are is much bigger than what you do.

I urge you to make peace with the possibility of failure, then begin to climb your impossible mountain, purely for the thrill of the climb. Don't worry about whether you'll ever reach the summit. It's really not important. Learn to celebrate each struggling step forward, always remembering, "I've never been this high before."

Are you ready to start climbing?

Chris Maddock tells me that reaching the summit of a mountain is a lot like finishing a good book. Just as the joy of a good book is never in the finishing of it, but in the reading, the thrill of climbing comes not at the summit, but in the climb.

Ah, but a man's reach
Should exceed his grasp
Or what's a heaven for?

Robert Browning,
in the poem "Andrea Del Sarto"

131

57

Will You Succeed by Accident?

If you insist on leaving your fate to the gods, then the gods will repay your weakness by having a grin or two at your expense. Should you fail to pilot your own ship, don't be surprised at what inappropriate port you will find yourself docked. The dull and prosaic will be granted adventures that will dice their central nervous systems like an onion, romantic dreamers will end up in the rope years. . . . The price of self-destiny is never cheap, and in certain situations it is unthinkable. But to achieve the marvelous, it is precisely the unthinkable that must be thought.

— Tom Robbins, *Jitterbug Perfume*

Are you waiting for your big break in life? Are you waiting for a chance event to suddenly make everything better? The truth is that most "fortunate accidents" are not really accidents at all. They happen as the direct result of hope, faith, and passion.

No, I'm not just being ethereal and ditzy. Keep reading.

When you imagine a thing that you desperately want to make happen, you create a three-dimensional reality in your mind. You see it as though it has already become real in the objective, fourth-dimensional reality of time.

That's when the whole universe seems to start working for you.

Neurologist Richard Cytowic explains this phenomenon marvelously in his book *The Man Who Tasted Shapes:*

Creative people are like a dog with a bone. They refuse to let go of an idea. They mull over the problem at their workbench as well as in the most mundane places. They chew on it just as a dog chews on the same old bone for hours. And just as the dog guards the bone safely between its paws when not actively chewing it, creative people nurture an idea even when not actively thinking about it. The true marks of creativity are (1) an ability to sense which problems are likely to yield results and so are worth tackling, (2) confidence that you can solve the problems that you single out for solution, and (3) a dogged persistence that keeps you going when others would give up. Creativity does not result from mysterious visions that come in dreams, or from fortuitous circumstances. Creativity and persistence are synonymous. Constantly thinking about the problem, consciously and unconsciously, maximizes the possibility that a chance occurrence is likely to be useful in solving it.

What do you want to make happen? The first step is to see it vividly in your mind. The second step is to cause all those around you to see it just as vividly in theirs.

Dreams are highly contagious.

What's yours? 🙠

Remember the admonition of Napoleon: "Small plans do not enflame the hearts of men." Dream large!

When a man has quietly made up his mind
that there is nothing he cannot endure,
his fears leave him.

Grove Patterson

58

Are You the Average American?

Rich people and poor people are exactly the same, except in one respect — rich people think rich.

— Herb Kay

A survey by Roper Starch Worldwide tells us that the average American believes he would need at least $25,000 a year "to get by," and that an annual income of $102,000 "would fulfill all dreams." When the same questions were posed to those with incomes in the top 1 percent of the nation, these heavy hitters reported that it would take $80,000 a year to get by, and $500,000 to fulfill all dreams. Upon reading this, your first response probably is to think, "The more a person has, the more he thinks he needs," but Herb Kay sees it a little differently. He says that rich people are rich *because* they think it takes $80,000 a year to get by.

The average American is average because he thinks average thoughts and does average things as a result.

Are you average? And if so, do you enjoy it?

Please understand that I'm not trying to be flip or condescending in any way. The shocking clarity of my cold questions springs from my deep belief that every person is uniquely gifted and that few joys are as great as discovering and using one's gift. The world is full of "average" people only because we have attempted to agree, as a group, on how success should be measured, and having thus conspired, we spend our lives following each other around in a tedious circle instead of following our individual hearts.

"The profoundest distances are never geographical."
— John Fowles

The average American gets average results and is paid average money for them, but no person can be average who has discovered and developed his gift.

What is your gift? ॐ

134

59

The Ear Is for More Than Listening

According to the Neurovestibular Adaptation Research Team of the National Space Biomedical Research Institute, approxiately 2 million Americans suffer chronic impairment from dizziness or have difficulty with balance. Eighty million of us have experienced problems with dizziness, and nearly a quarter of all emergency room visits include a complaint of dizziness.

It's interesting that the cause of dizziness is located near the auditory cortex and Broca's area of the brain. We tend to think of the ear as the organ for hearing, but in addition to the structures that are used for hearing, the inner ear contains the utriculus and the sacculus, the chief organs of balance and orientation.

Balance and orientation are as important emotionally as they are physically. Without physical balance and orientation, you cannot function in four-dimensional reality, the objective space-time continuum. Without emotional balance and orientation, you cannot function in three-dimensional reality, the private reality of your mind, your will, and your emotions.

Spin in a circle, ride a radical roller coaster, or hold your breath for too long and you'll lose your sense of balance. To regain it, you must be still for awhile.

Day after day, you've been spinning in an ever-tightening circle of opportunity and obligation, fantasy and fun. You've been riding life's roller coaster while holding your breath for a long time now.

Is it time for you to be still? ❧

Fear is silence, and if you face the silence and listen to it and go through it, you eventually come to a dark place of deeper peace.

— Ian Macleod,
Tirkiluk

60

Look Out the Other Window

When Princess Pennie was a little girl, she worried about growing old with a husband. It's not that she feared losing her youth or beauty; her gnawing concern was "After ten or twenty years together, what will we have left to talk about?"

I've been smiling to myself about Pennie's childhood fear since last Friday, when she asked during lunch, "How do you do it?" (This year we're celebrating our twenty-fifth wedding anniversary.) I answered, "Do what?" and she replied, "Leave all the cares of the office at the office. I've never been able to do it."

When I told her my secret, she cocked her head and said, "You really need to send our subscribers a Monday Morning Memo about that. I don't think most people have ever thought about it that way."

At lunch the following Sunday, our good friend Akintunde was saying that he hadn't been able to unwind for several weeks because he couldn't get his mind off all his troubles and urgent deadlines at work. It seems that Akintunde is programming a new video game for Nintendo, and the game keeps inexplicably crashing. He looked at me and asked, "So how do you do it?"

I glanced at Pennie. She was smiling.

Pointing to the east, I said, "Look out that window and tell me what you see." Akintunde looked intently out the window and described in detail what he saw there. "Now look out this window," I said, pointing to the west, "and tell me what you see." Akintunde spent the next several moments describing an entirely different scene.

I said, "That's how I do it."

When he didn't understand, I pointed to a bare wall and said, "Tell me what you see."

Akintunde said, "I see nothing but a blank wall."

"Keep looking," I told him. After a minute of watching him stare silently at the wall, I asked, "Are you thinking about what you saw out the window?"

"Yes, I am," he laughed. "How did you know?"

"Akintunde," I said, "if you will pour yourself into something that will occupy your evenings and weekends as completely as your job occupies your nine to five, you'll find that you will soon be feeling less tired, less frustrated, and less stressed out about what's happening at the office. The reason you can't quit thinking about the office is because you're going home each night and staring at the wall."

Akintunde looked like a man who had just been given permission to live. "I'm going to study grackles!" he shouted. "I've really been wanting to, but I thought it would just make me more tired."

"Study grackles," we told him. Pennie and I fully expect Akintunde Omitowoju to become the world's foremost authority on grackles.

Like most people, our friend Akintunde had been confusing rest with idleness. Rest is not idleness. Rest is simply looking out a different window. If you have a job, or anything else that you struggle with and worry about, you have a window that looks to the east.

But do you have one that looks to the west? ◦঵

There is no cure for birth or death save to enjoy the interval.

— George Santayana

61

"This Is My Back"

by Rex Williams

Are you as successful as you would like to be right now? If you are, then stop reading, go away, and leave the rest of us alone to look at what we have, what we want, and how we're going to get it. (Yes, I'm talking some pretty big talk, but I can do that because I'm only 20, okay?)

I've decided that whatever I do in life, I'm going to be huge. I'll be either a huge success or a huge failure. Sure, having only the success would be nice, but I also know that I can't become a huge success unless I'm willing to lose what little I already have. I've got to be willing live in my car for a while if I screw up. And I've got to be prepared not to flinch when I'm laughed at a couple of hundred times for moronic decisions. But no one will ever doubt my determination to pull my foot from my mouth, stand back up, and try one more time. They won't doubt it, because they will have seen me do it.

How much embarrassment are you willing to risk?

Although hugeness is in my future, I won't be the least bit surprised if I plummet back down to Earth in a fiery ball of bad choices. (Perhaps my inflated ego will cushion the landing.) This is what few businesspeople realize: if you were successful once, you can do it again.

If you try to get success in a headlock, all you'll really be doing is choking the creativity and life from your company. That's not what you want, is it?

Often when people become successful, they lose their willingness to accept risk. Ironically, it was usually taking a chance that made them successful in the first place. But once they actually have something to lose, the term "It's all or nothing" seems a little less valiant and a lot more foolish.

Rex Williams is a scion of the Wizard and Princess Pennie.

Putting everything on the line, however, isn't for everyone. If you have a spouse, 2.7 kids, and a mortgage, then to throw your kids' college fund into a risky scheme is to walk the fine line between audacious and asinine.

You can't take over the world by putting a new coffee machine on the main floor or having a "50% Off Sale!" every other Tuesday. You've got to make choices that will have those around you asking with furrowed brow, "What the hell was he thinking?" But once your idea is working and the money's rolling in, you can do the happy dance right in front of them.

Have you seen the commercial for the Special Olympics? A mentally challenged boy is shown walking up to people, pointing behind him, and saying, "This is my back. This is my back." At the end of the commercial he says, "It's the only thing you're going to see when we race." That boy is my hero. Shaking off the business herd mentality and doing things that fly in the face of everyone else's negative feedback takes a lot of guts.

Be confident, audacious, maybe even a little egotistical. Do you have the audacity to say and do the things that can make you huge? If you want to be considered a genius, you must be willing to look like a fool.

I certainly am. Are you?

Courage is the human virtue that counts most — courage to act on limited knowledge and insufficient evidence. That's all any of us have.

Robert Frost

62

Which Buffett?

You've won a contest. You get to hang out for a week with someone named Buffett. "So tell me," the voice on the phone asks, "do you want to 'invest' your week with Warren or 'spend' it with Jimmy? Which Buffett do you choose?"

Warren Buffet is the billionaire chairman of Berkshire Hathaway, an investment company whose stock sells for about $40,000 a share on a bad day, $75,000 on a good day. What you might learn from Warren Buffett in a week! (At the very least, imagine how his name would look as a reference on your résumé.)

Jimmy Buffett, on the other hand, is the mayor of Margaritaville. You can sing that one, can't you? "Blew out my flip flop, stepped on a pop top; cut my heel, had to cruise on back home. But there's booze in the blender, and soon it will render, that frozen concoction that helps me hang on. . . ." A week with Jimmy Buffett would have you swimming in Caribbean memories for a lifetime.

Hmmm. . . . Isn't this the story of the grasshopper and the ant? "The ant works in the oppressive heat all summer, fortifying his house against the elements and storing supplies to last the winter, while the foolish grasshopper just laughs and plays and dances the summer away. When winter comes, the ant is warm and well fed, while the grasshopper shivers and starves out in the cold. The end." You enjoy prosperity, but there's also a voice whispering in your ear: "Remember, if you win the rat race, you're still a rat."

Which Buffett would you choose?

The good news is that you never have to make that kind of choice. In the game of life, you get to make up your own rules. "Hey, how about if I work five or six days with Warren and then go spend a day or two acting silly with Jimmy?" The voice at the other end of the line says, "Work for five or six days and then rest for one or two? Sounds like a good plan. How did you come up with that?" You answer, "I read it somewhere." "Sounds like a good book," the voice replies. "Yeah, I think maybe I've heard it called that before."

The great essentials of happiness are something to do, something to love, and something to hope for.

Unknown

63

Moonshadow Medicine

It's important that you know How and When to do the Huckleberry Finn. . . .

Ray Bard is the founder of Bard Press, widely considered to be the most prestigious publisher of business books in America. Like you and me, Ray Bard lives a frantic, hurly-burly life with far too much to do and too little time. Recently, Ray clicked my e-mail address by mistake and I was treated to a rare insight into the mind of a powerful publisher. My only question is this: "Who is Maria?"

Maria,

Back today and swamped. . . . Sorry to be so long getting back to you.

On Tuesday I woke up and asked myself, "Do I have to go to work today?". . . the answer was "no." Ate a quick bite of breakfast, pointed my auto west. One advantage of living on the eastern edge of the Texas Hill Country is that when you head west, you're almost immediately in "The West," and can feel the spirit of the space.

There is an old used bookstore about 200 miles away in a town called San Angelo, where stacks and stacks of books from one doorway to another lead to little, crowded rooms packed with tomes from the past. Those books were calling me.

The Texas Hill Country is full of rolling hills, live oaks, cedars, rocks of all sizes, and lots of livestock, with the occasional human here and there. Most towns have seen their day . . . shriveling in the hot sun . . . peeling paint on the houses, some vacant, some not.

I stop for gas in tiny Eden, which has a new penal facility — Texas is big on locking up folks who use nasty drugs and do other things that offend sensible people — then pass through booming Brady, pop. 5,946, which is getting ready for its annual World Championship Goat BBQ contest on Labor Day weekend. As I get closer to San Angelo, the Hill Country begins to turn into farm country . . . long rows of cotton, all green and alive, as far as the eye can see on this flatland fed with water gushing forth from hundreds of feet below the surface.

Soon arrived at my old haunt. Talked awhile about the Wild West with the bookstore owner, then asked him where I could find the best chicken-fried steak in town. He directed me to the Dunbar Café. Sure enough, a sweet, red-haired beauty wearing blue jeans and a big smile brought me two huge slabs of breaded beef with lots of gravy on the side. At the end I was "plumb full," but was somehow able to manage a slice of their homemade coconut cream pie.

One of the things that wandering off like this does is to let me see how the rest of the world lives. How that cordial waitress treats everyone like we are really being served. An old couple, barely able to walk, joins the bustle of the place, looking for their usual table. My red-haired angel of country Epicurean delights treats them really special, making sure their every need is catered to . . . their wish is her command.

The sun is still up and I'm hankering for the wide-open spaces again, so I head south to see how far I can make it before it's time to pull over for the evening. Local travelers in pickup trucks, old beat-up autos from Detroit (not many foreign cars out here), and clean Cadillacs wave a greeting as they approach. Usually just a forefinger raised off the steering wheel or some other small signal that says "howdy." An important protocol of the road out West.

I'm about out of gas (me, not my auto) by the time I hit the city limits of El Dorado (pop. 2,019). The Shaw Motel (only one in town) has a Vacancy sign lit so I pull in. The squeaky screen door to the office leads me to a small registration window that has an old-fashioned ringer on the side. I push the white button and it goes zzz . . . zzz. . . . A little white-haired lady, no more than four feet tall and at least eighty years old, appears and gently offers me her evening greeting. I, in my best West Texas manner, offer her the same and inquire about the cost of lodging at her fine place. She replies "Twenty-five dollars and forty-nine cents." I say, "Mighty fine," and fish my money clip out of my pocket (people out here are partial to cash). She offers a receipt, which I decline. As I head out the door, key in hand, she tells me to be sure to let her know if there's anything that I need. I tell her thanks, but that I'm pretty sure I've found what I needed.

Ray Bard

You'll never know how hard it was to get permission from Ray to print this....

64

Big Questions, Little Answers

When Debra Dinnocenzo and Rick Swegan first began planning their book *DotCalm,* they asked if I would answer some survey questions for them. When their questions arrived, I thought, "These are some really great questions. I'll be anxious to read other people's responses to them." For the curious, here are the questions they asked, along with my answers:

Q: What techniques do you use to balance all the demands of your life and work?

A: I'm not sure "balance" is the right word, as it implies fair and equal treatment of all obligations. I think perhaps a better word is "prioritize." I believe that the key to maintaining one's sanity today is the ability to separate the truly important from the merely urgent. The question that you must continually ask yourself is "What, exactly, are the consequences of NOT doing this?" A couple of years ago I received a summons to jury duty that informed me that I was required BY LAW to appear at a certain place at a certain time. I said, "I wonder what happens if I don't show up? Do they send a police officer to my door? Do they mail me a nasty note saying that I'm a bad American? Do they kick my cocker spaniel?" I ignored the summons and nothing happened. (Yes, I am a bad person.)

Q: How do you limit your accessibility to avoid interruptions to personal time?

A: Neither my clients nor my staff know my home phone number or my cell phone number. When I'm not at the office, I'm not at work. Walking out the door each night, I make peace with my decision to quit for the day by saying, "Let worlds collide, let millions die. I've done all I can." The next day when I arrive at the office and find that planets did not collide and millions did not die as a result of my having left a few things undone, I happily get back to work.

Q: How do you completely disconnect from work?

A: I aggressively pursue things that I think are interesting. I research, read, go shopping, and repair stuff. Pennie (my wife and business partner) and I have a rule that we never discuss the office at home. Never.

Q: How do you unwind, reenergize, and renew your spirit/energy?

A: Waking up curious in the middle of the night, I write. It's now 3:41 AM.

Q: How do you maintain a sense of community and real human contact?

A: Each day, I leave and eat lunch outside the office, usually somewhere quiet and with cloth napkins. It's my rule never to eat alone and always to pick up the tab. I believe that outside of marriage there is little human contact as intimate as sharing a meal with someone in a quiet place.

Q: How do you manage the barrage of e-mail, voice mail, and information that exists?

A: I respond to only two or three inquiries per day, but each of these receives a full and complete response from me. Today, I am responding to you. The senders of the other 162 e-mails currently on my desktop will either assume that I'm rude, or that I don't care, or that I'm too busy to respond. I can't change what they think. Neither can I put more hours on the clock. I believe that the people most likely to lie awake at night are the ones who feel they must answer the telephone every time it rings, type responses to every e-mail, and make return calls to every caller who leaves a message. May the Lord have pity on those poor souls. . . . Amen.

Q: How does the organization you work for help or hinder you in achieving focus and balance?

A: I don't believe that an organization can help, or hinder, the individual in his search for personal peace. Contentment is not drawn from a person's circumstances or surroundings. Anyone who believes his employer can contribute to, or detract from, his sense of well-being is probably going to live a life without it. Peace comes from the inside, not the outside.

Now do you see what I was saying about the questions being interesting?

© Clayton J. Price

65

An Old Mustang Revertible

I have a 1971 Mustang with a canvas top that folds down behind the rear seat. Ask me why I chose to restore this particular year, make, and model of car, and I'll immediately point out to you the convenience of having a gas cap that is centered between the tail lights. "You can pull up on either side of the gas pump. Either side!" After showing you how effortlessly one can remove the gas cap, I'll continue, as though you're actually interested, "And it's not hidden behind an irritating, spring-loaded license plate like the gas caps on GM cars!" By the time I've explained the slope angle of the windshield and pointed out the fully retractable wipers, you'll be wishing you had never asked.

But Pennie will tell you that the real reason we own a '71 Mustang is because every time I sit in one, I go back in time to when I was fifteen years old. That was the year Perry McKee and I ruled the world from our headquarters on the second floor of his grandmother's house in Muskogee, Oklahoma.

Perry always drove the Mustang with his left hand, because his right hand was busy pounding invisible piano keys on the dash as we sang at the top of our lungs to a blaring AM radio. And in between each song, we'd lean out the windows and shout, "Suuuu-bah-RUUUUUU!"

Perry and I never once lost a race in that Mustang. Never. But then, none of the other drivers ever knew that they had been racing. Like the shark in the movie *Jaws,* our Mustang was just a speck in their rear-view mirrors, right up until the moment Perry and I zipped past them with shouts of "SubahRUUU!" It was always then that Perry would turn to me and say, "Got 'em!"

If a girl was especially pretty or a cheeseburger was particularly good, Perry and I would lock eyes for a moment, turn one thumb slowly upward, and say in solemn unison, "Subaru."

When we got tired of sitting at a red light, we'd throw our fingertips toward it and shout the command, "Subaru!" Shortly thereafter, the light would always turn green.

Why "Subaru"? Well, in simple truth, Perry and I just liked the sound of the word.

And when you rule the world, that's the only reason you need.

Anyone without a sense of humor is at the mercy of everyone else.

William Rostler

66

Personal, Permanent, & Pervasive

It comes down to a simple choice — get busy living or get busy dying.

— Andy Dufresne, in *The Shawshank Redemption*

When something bad happens, is it usually your fault, or is it someone else's? Will the results of the adversity be temporary or permanent? Will it spread to other areas of your life, or will it be it limited to a single area?

According to Dr. Martin Seligman of the Center for Applied Cognitive Studies, optimists and pessimists are easily identified through their explanations of adversity and success. The principal differences in their respective outlooks revolve around the issues of personalization, permanence, and pervasiveness.

When adversity happens, the pessimist thinks, "It's my fault (personalization). It's gonna last forever (permanence), and it will affect every area of my life (pervasiveness)." Whereas the optimist believes, "It's someone else's fault. It's only temporary, and it won't affect other areas of my life."

When success happens however, the explanations are reversed. The pessimist believes, "Someone else made it happen. It won't last, and it won't help me in any other area of my life." The optimist, on the other hand, believes the same things about success that the pessimist believes about adversity! "I made it happen (personalization). This is one in a line of many successes (permanence), and the effect will ripple throughout my life (pervasiveness)."

Does it surprise you to learn that pessimists explain adversity in exactly the same way that optimists explain success?

How do you explain adversity and success?

"Hope is a good thing, maybe the best of things. And no good thing ever dies."

— Andy Dufresne, in
The Shawshank Redemption

67

Dark Water, Strong Current

Alone or in public, when something good happens and I'm happy, I do a perfectly ridiculous little dance. Pennie calls it my "dance of delight." It makes me look like an idiot.

I don't care.

By doing the dance when I'm feeling great, I turn it into a powerful tool I can use when I sense the ominous darkness that occasionally tries to creep over my soul. Do you know the darkness I mean? That desolate blues of midnight, "nothing matters" sort of darkness that tries to pull you downward into a whirlpool of despair? (Some of you have no idea what I'm talking about. You're very fortunate. But if, like me, you occasionally feel that darkness, nod your head.)

I do the dance when I'm happy because I want to store the physical feel of it as an associative memory closely linked to good news, sunny skies, serendipity, and joy. Then, when I need to feel those feelings, all I have to do is dance my little dance to recall them. The dance of delight is my first weapon against the blues.

If my dance isn't enough to chase the blues away, I'll walk into the offices of my co-workers and pay each of them a genuine, heartfelt compliment. This technique is a tough one because it requires you to say warm, positive things at a time when you least feel like saying them, but after you've made four or five other people feel like a million bucks, you're usually feeling pretty darn good yourself.

The blues usually come on me as a result of spending too much time thinking about myself, my circumstances, my problems, disappointments, and anxieties. Let me say it plainly: Focus on making yourself happy and you'll soon be miserable. Focus on bringing joy to others and your own happiness will quickly follow. To beat the blues, you've got to redirect your emotional river from inward-flowing to outward-flowing.

When the river of blues is flowing so deep and fast that I can no longer turn it around, I don't swim against the current; I find someone else to encourage. I do this because we learn what we believe as we hear ourselves say it. And when you're deep in the blues, you need to remember what you believe.

Half a century ago, Dr. Leon Festinger paid sixty people to participate in what he told them was to be "a study of hand-eye coordination." None of the sixty participants ever met. They took the tests at different times on different days. During the "test," each participant was asked to aimlessly move wooden pegs around on a board while seated in a room alone. After half an hour, an assistant would enter the room and announce that the test was over. As participants exited the building, a second assistant would present them with a score sheet asking them to honestly rate how interesting they had found the task to be. The first thirty participants ranked the task as the most boring thing they had ever done.

The next thirty participants were treated exactly the same as the first thirty, except that each was told by the assistant at the end of the half-hour, "We're having trouble getting subjects for the tests, so if on your way out, you could mention to the next candidate that you found the test to be interesting, it would really help us a lot." The assistant then opened the door and introduced the participant to a person of his own age who, he was told, was the next candidate. (It was actually a staff member.) Shaking the stranger's hand, the participant would say something like "It's really a very interesting test" or "I found it to be quite fascinating." After meeting and encouraging the "candidate," he exited to the outer lobby where the second assistant gave him the same score sheet that each of the first thirty had received.

Does it surprise you to learn that the second thirty, those who filled out the score sheets immediately after hearing themselves say, "It was interesting," rated the task far more highly than the first thirty?

How we feel is greatly influenced by what we say.

What have you been hearing yourself say lately? 🙿

68

"... a Doctor or a Lawyer"

Never ridicule a beginner lest you kill talent before it develops.

— Knute Rockne

For every doctor who graduated at the top of his class, there is another one who graduated at the bottom. Dead last. Barely made it through medical school. Most likely the unlucky offspring of parents who decided their child was "going to be a doctor or a lawyer" before the poor kid was even born.

Why do parents do this?

Our younger son, Jake, was telling Pennie and me about a friend at school whose parents were angry with him because he signed up to be on the debate team instead of the football team. According to them, their son had made a horrible mistake "that will adversely affect the rest of his life."

Call me stupid. Call me a bad parent. Disagree with me violently if you'd like, but I've instructed my boys to study whatever they find interesting. "Live your own life and let others live theirs," is my advice to them and to you.

Now are you ready to hear the really shocking part? I honestly don't care if my boys go to college or not. "If there's something you guys want to study, I'll pay for it. If you want to start a little business, I'll help you. If you don't want to do either of these, then try to find a job working for someone you really like. And be sure to marry your best friend."

Win the lottery and be happy for a year. Do what you love and be happy for life.

"What do you want to be when you grow up?" is probably the most often asked question in the world. But has there ever been a kid who could answer it? I still don't know what I want to be when I grow up. Do you? (Is it our own indecision on the subject that drives us to ask this question of every child we meet?)

The next time you're tempted to ask a child what he wants to be when he grows up, here are the questions I hope you'll ask instead: "What kinds of things are you curious about? Have you learned anything interesting today? What have you seen or heard that makes you go 'Hmm. . .'?"

Ask the questions. I dare you. The answers you get will rock your world.

155

69

Stray and Random Thoughts

Each week without fail, I receive at least one fax or e-mail asking, "What is your process for planning and research? Can you tell me how to do it?" Certainly. It's a very simple, four-step system:

1. Always carry a pen in your left front pants pocket.

2. Anytime you see, hear, or think an interesting thought, write it down.

3. Each morning about 4:30 AM, dig through the pockets of your dirty clothes and read all the notes you wrote to yourself the previous day.

4. If any of the notes sparks an interest, dig into it and start writing. If not, go back to bed.

Here's what I found in my pockets this morning:

Life is short. So make fun of it.

While in Guatemala, remember to ask Sergio, Guillermo, and Juan Manuel for suggestions about what to give as the Garcia Brothers Award at Wizard Academy.

Have Chris research parallels between the laws that govern the space/time continuum and the failure of businesses (most recently dotcoms) due to unrealistic ramp-up projections in their business plans. In photography, "foreshortening" makes things look closer than they really are. Does this change the distance? No. Does it change the amount of time required to cover the distance? No. Will a foreshortened time horizon cause us to make bad decisions in business? Yes. You cannot exceed the speed of light. Ask Chris to find business parallels for mass, gravity, time, distance, light speed, terminal velocity, etc.

Consider evangelical implications of Sean McNally's statement, "Darkness is not the opposite of light. It is the absence of it."

Remember to thank Dick Taylor. Also the nice couple that own the juice bars in Portland. Thank Roy Laughlin for Michael J. Gelb's *How to Think Like Leonardo da Vinci.* (Also buy copies for staff.) Get digital camera recommendation from Rich. Thank Alex Benningfield for his gift of the door from the General Lee.

Buy additional copies of *Interaction of Color* by Josef Albers. Page 3: "If one says 'Red' and there are 50 people listening, it can be expected that there will be 50 reds in their minds. And one can be sure that all these reds will be very different. Even when a certain color is specified which all listeners have seen innumerable times — such as the red of the Coca-Cola signs, which is the same red all over the country — they will still think of many different reds. Even if the listeners have hundreds of reds in front of them from which to choose the Coca-Cola red, they will again select quite different colors. It is hard, if not impossible, to remember distinct colors. This underscores the important fact that visual memory is very poor in comparison with our auditory memory." Page 68: "It seems worthwhile to distinguish 3 basically different approaches to color based upon the different interests of the physicist, the psychologist, and the colorist. Whereas the primary colors for the colorist (painters, designers) are yellow-red-blue, the physicist has 3 other primaries (not including yellow), and the psychologist counts 4 primaries (the 4th being green), plus 2 neutrals, white and black."

Learn about Munsell color system. Locate and purchase additional copies of *Language and Working Memory* by Dr. Alan Baddeley. ❧

Only twice in my life have I ever awarded anyone the pen out of my left front pocket. The first went to Juan Manuel Garcia and the second was given to Tom Pelton. But those are stories for another day. I do need to remember to write those stories, though. ... Maybe I should stick a note in my pocket.

70

Experience Must First Be a Verb

Employers are searching for people with experience, not so much because these people will know what to do, but because they will know what not to do — a valuable thing to know, learned best by doing it. The experience that you see listed as a noun on today's résumé was but yesterday a verb, something that actually happened.

Today's wisdom comes from yesterday's mistakes. A person who is not making mistakes is someone who is not taking chances, someone who is trying no new things. Such a person is tragically average at best. You'll have to look elsewhere to find innovation, daring, and genius.

Call me crazy, but I agree with Oscar Wilde, who said, "An idea that is not dangerous is not worthy of being called an idea at all. Experience is the name everyone gives to his mistakes."

I think Oscar was saying, "Follow a trail of crazy mistakes and at the end of them you'll find a genius."

You hear a lot of brave talk these days about employee empowerment. Unfortunately, what most companies are calling "empowerment" is really just an increase in employee responsibility without a commensurate increase in authority. Most employers are anxious to dole out responsibility, but few are eager to pay for their employees' mistakes.

Do you want to dominate your category? The first step is to hire talented people who have no experience doing what you need them to do. Train these people, knowing full well that you will soon be called upon to cheerfully pay for all their mistakes. It may prove to be the best investment you ever made.

During the first hour of their first day on the job, my friend Richard Kessler tells every new employee, "When you're helping a customer of this company, always remember that you ARE the company. When a decision needs to be made, make it. Do what you believe is right. Nine times out of ten, you're going to make a fabulous decision. One time in ten, I'm going to wish that you had done something different. Backing you up on those decisions is the price that I'm willing to pay to get the other nine decisions from you. Never, ever be afraid to do what you truly believe is right."

What would living in America be like if everyone worked for Richard Kessler?

"The moment you let avoiding failure become your motivator, you're down the path of inactivity. You can only stumble if you're moving. If you don't have a few failures, you're not taking enough chances. Nobody can be right all the time, and the big companies didn't become big by playing it safe."

— Coca-Cola chairman Roberto Goizueta, after the "New Coke" debacle of 1985

Good judgment comes from experience, and experience . . . well, experience comes from poor judgment.

Cousin Woodman

71

Wonkus Is as Wonkus Does

(On the Trail of the Wizard's Beagle)

The first time I ever used the word "wonkus" was in an e-mail to a magazine editor, Ed Ryan, who immediately replied, "Wonkus?" As I was typing the answer, "I don't know, I just made it up," the beagle in my brain smelled a rabbit and bolted off into the woods after it.

Thank God for Google.com. "Search: wonkus." After searching more than one billion, three hundred forty-six million, nine hundred sixty-six thousand web pages, Google was able to find only ten uses of "wonkus."

The fact that a couple of writers had used "wonkus" as a slang term for a certain part of the male anatomy didn't surprise me, since half the words in the English language have been used that way. It was the other eight uses of "wonkus" that proved interesting.

In a short story called "Xena and the Chocolate Factory," Snoopmeff@aol.com wraps up her parody of ancient Greek gods and goddesses with the following:

> Joxer was in a horrible accident involving something in the factory and was ripped to pieces. His friend Willae Wonkus now runs the factory. Snoop went back to her own time and is still trying to figure out how to play the blues on a *$&%@ panflute.

In his review of the CD *Dream after a Large Lunch*, Derek Kipp uses "wonkus" as part of the Latin name for a particular species of imaginary animal:

> As any species grows more prolific — any species, really, but here we're talking about the effusive, sometimes elusive, Jazzus Wonkus — maintaining uniqueness and distinguishing oneself can be a difficult thing indeed.

See ch. 54, "The Beagle in Your Brain."

In *The Adventures of Worldwalking Ritch*, by "Jesse," also known as the "Great Banana," we read,

> There is a story about a man who woke up one morning as a giant purple wonkus, one of the rarest creatures in the known universe, and all his wife said to him was "Go back to bed, love. You look terrible." However, wonki don't come into our story yet.

Evidently, the plural of wonkus is wonki.
On a website recognizing Harry Potter fans, we find:

> Tony Meizelis . . . for providing two of the best "How I Got Hooked on Harry" stories ever, for a wealth of ideas, and for Wonkus Intellectullus, the disaffected Phoenix.

(The Phoenix was a legendary bird that was consumed by fire, only to rise from its own ashes more beautiful than before.)
And then there was the mysterious foreign language entry:

> Namnet kommer från det indianska ordet Wonkus, som betyder "Räven." Uncas varen mäktig hövding över moheganerna under den första koloniala tiden i New. . . .

On May 22, 1998, Donna E. Shalala addressed the graduates of Georgetown University's Public Policy Institute as follows:

> I want to thank the students of this Institute for the privilege of addressing your Tropaia. You've chosen a profession whose chief currency is words — lots of words. I'll try to keep mine brief because I know the only thing standing between you and the real world . . . is me and my speech. But as you step across the threshold today, the good news and the bad news are that henceforth and forever you shall be known throughout the land as a member of that unique species known as *Publicus consilium wonkus*. The policy wonk.

Does it amaze you, as it does me, that virtually all who pulled the word "wonkus" from the mists of their own imagination used it as the name of an animal? People somehow seem to sense that a wonkus is a living thing and not an inanimate object. (Hmm . . . the beagle lays his head on his paws for a nice long think.) Finally, when I found the "real" answer in a 1965 book called *Oklahoma Place Names,* by George H. Fhirk, the beagle and I were stunned: "Uncas — in Kay County, 6 miles west of Kaw. A post office from June 21, 1895 to May 31, 1956. Named for Uncas, Mohegan chief. The word 'uncas' is from 'wonkus,' meaning 'fox.'"

The last Google.com entry was a discussion about the current state of web site design. Tom said, "I can't imagine that anybody ever thought they weren't planning to take that bottom dollar. Am I missing something?" To which Zvi Gilbert replied, "If you're critiquing mass society, then feeding from the hand that you bite is wonkus." (According to Gilbert's use of it, the word "wonkus" can also mean "crazy.")

Just then I remembered the age-old expression, "crazy like a fox." Whoa. . . . Isn't this when Rod Serling is supposed to step out from *The Twilight Zone* and say in that inimitable voice of his: "Consider if you will . . . the wonkus"? ◈

Wow,
A wonkus
really IS
an animal.

Part the Fourth

Wizards at Large

In Which the Wizard Recounts Tales of Persons Exemplifying the Principles upon Which Wizardry Is Founded

72

Think Big, Start Small

People frustrate me. For all their talk about being "goal oriented," most people either aren't willing to dream big enough, or they're not willing to start small enough. Maybe I'm being harsh, but it seems to me that most "goal-oriented" people just sit around sighing wistfully, "If only. . . ."

I suspect the problem with the first group, the ones who aren't willing to dream big enough, is the fear of failure. These people are afraid to dream big dreams because they fear the disappointment that might follow should their grand dreams fail to come true. The problem with the second group, the ones who aren't willing to start small enough, is ego. They just can't understand how volunteering to teach a Sunday school class of fifth graders can be the vital first step toward a career as a highly paid public speaker. Their big egos won't let them do the small thing that is currently within their power to do. They refuse to believe that every great success must necessarily begin with a sad, pathetic, laughable first attempt. These are the people we see sighing and waiting for their "big break."

What about you? What steps are you taking to move yourself toward your dream? If your dream is to write the Great American Novel, then I suggest that you start writing, and when you're done, pay the corner print shop to print a few hundred copies to give away to anyone who's willing to read what you've written. If your dream is to sing before an audience of thousands, then start by singing to your family and friends. Yes, they're going to laugh at you. Get over it. When you start getting compliments and looks of surprise, go find someone who owns some multitrack recording equipment and pay him to record your act. Then pass out free CDs and cassettes of your performance to anyone who will listen to them. Are you beginning to get the idea here?

One of the wisest men I know, Dan Davis, once said, "Anything worth doing is worth doing badly. You will never be able to do a thing better until first you've done it badly. If a thing is worth doing, it's worth doing."

There is no place to start other than where you are. And one thing is certain; you are where you are. All that remains is for you to get up and get started down the road that will take you to wherever it is you're going.

As my friend Tony says, "Pull the trigger and ride the bullet." If the first bullet misses the target, then pull the trigger and ride another one. The game isn't over until you decide you don't want to play anymore.

So what are you going to do now?

When I was a young man I observed that nine out of ten things I did were failures. I didn't want to be a failure, so I did ten times more work.

George Bernard Shaw

73

Right Where You Are

James Cramer dreams of managing a multimillion-dollar stock portfolio. He wants to be a force on Wall Street and speak with a voice of thunder.

James Cramer barely makes a living as a writer for a small newspaper.

Since he has zero real dollars to invest, James begins managing an imaginary stock portfolio. Soon he is spending all his free time studying the stock market and agonizing over his imaginary investments as though millions of real dollars were at stake. His focus and intensity are astounding. His friends ask, "What's gotten into James?"

James is bursting with new theories about stock trading. Since his newspaper bosses won't let him write about his bizarre ideas, he decides simply to start where he's at. So, like a dreamer, James Cramer begins leaving stock tips on his answering machine for whoever might happen to call his number.

Sometimes the calls are from telemarketers who want James to change his long-distance service. Sometimes the calls are from strangers who have mistakenly dialed the wrong number. But mostly the calls are from friends who think James is tilting at windmills. "Listen, Don Quixote, I'm really sick of having to listen to your stupid stock-tip-of-the-day before I can leave you a message. Just cut it out, okay? No one is interested, and even if we were, you know that none of us has any money. Hey, call me when you get in and we'll decide where to have dinner. But I don't want to hear about the stock market tonight, okay? And by the way, you're an idiot."

Martin Peretz wants James to write a book review for his magazine, *The New Republic.* He calls and gets the answering machine. Fascinated by the stock tip, Peretz decides to take the advice that James has so generously left for "whosoever will." Soon Peretz is a daily caller. One day he calls while James is at home. There's an awkward silence while he waits for the recording to begin. When Peretz finally realizes that James is actually on the line, he says, "Hi. My name is Martin Peretz, and I'm convinced that your stock tips are way better than what I'm getting from my stockbroker. How would you like to manage a $500,000 portfolio?"

No, this is not a story that I invented for a movie script. James Cramer and Martin Peretz are both real people. Today, James Cramer is a hurricane on Wall Street, where he manages a stock portfolio that exceeds $200 million. His website, www.TheStreet.com, is visited by thousands of investors each day.

Maybe James Cramer's friends were right: only an idiot would do that much research just to leave a daily stock tip on an answering machine. Yes, any person who would do that would have to be a solid gold, totally focused, two-hundred-million-dollar idiot.

Gosh, I wish I were that big an idiot.

Honor begins with accepting that
what we do, large or small, matters.

James Webb

7

74

"Never Had a Chance"

The inevitable is only that which we do not resist.

— Justice Louis Brandeis

Orphaned at the age of seven, she's a black, self-made millionaire who offers powerful advice to all who will listen. "There is no royal flower-strewn path to success," she once commented, "and if there is, I've not found it. If I have accomplished anything in life, it is because I have been willing to work hard." To teenagers she says, "Don't sit and wait for opportunities to come. You have to get up and make them." But it's on the subject of civil rights that her voice rings out most clearly: "America doesn't respect anything but money. What our people need is a few millionaires."

Her magnificent, thirty-room Italian Renaissance mansion was designed by one of the world's leading architects, and its name, "Villa Lewaro," was given to it by Enrico Caruso, the legendary opera singer. Obviously, this is a woman of extraordinary elegance, wealth, and taste.

Can you name our black female millionaire? I'll give you a clue: she died exactly four years before television was invented. Now that sort of shoots your Oprah theory all to pieces, doesn't it? No, the great opera singer Enrico Caruso wasn't just an historical figure to Sarah Breedlove, he was a personal friend, and Sarah wasn't just America's first black female millionaire. She was America's first self-made female millionaire, period.

Born in 1867 on a Louisiana plantation, Sarah was the daughter of former slaves who died when she was seven. When Sarah was eighteen, she had a baby girl. Her husband died two years later. Yes, the woman who would become known throughout the world as

Madam C. J. Walker began her long walk toward fame and fortune as a black, twenty-year-old widow with a two-year-old baby on her arm. And she did it during a time when America was not only violently racist, but deeply sexist as well.

"I got my start by giving myself a start," she says. "I came from the cotton fields of the South. I was promoted from there to the washtub. Then I was promoted to the cook kitchen. And from there I promoted myself into the business of manufacturing cosmetics. Everybody told me I was making a mistake."

Evidently, everybody was wrong.

How about you? Do you have the patience, tenacity, and grit to bang the hammer of hard work against the anvil of your disadvantages until you've pounded your future into a shape that you like? Or do you just plan to sit there with your fingers crossed and wait for your "big break" and then, when it doesn't come, whine about how you "never had a chance"?

Man is a creature of hope and invention, both of which belie the idea that things cannot be changed.

Tom Clancy, *Debt of Honor*

75

Priorities

ames Cramer, the guy you met a few pages ago who started a multibillion-dollar consulting firm by leaving free stock tips on his answering machine, gave me permission to reprint this note he wrote to his friends. I think you'll like it.

All hell broke loose for me yesterday. I had so many crises going on that I could barely keep track of them. It is always difficult for me when I am out of the office. But yesterday I had to be at the office, at CNBC, for Squawk Box, at the Spy Bar to film a commercial for TheStreet.com, monitor my stocks — all of which were going down — and get this piece out.

At 2 PM I was juggling two cell phones and my personal computer, while a woman put makeup on my face and a guy tied a tie around my neck. Suddenly, Jeff, my partner, says, "call your wife at home, there's a problem."

I call, and sure enough our daughter is sick and has to be rushed to the hospital. Dehydration.

I say to my wife that I'd love to help out but I've got thirty people waiting on me at the commercial site, and two companies begging for me to do several things at once.

She says, okay. Do what you have to do. And I hang up.

And then it hits me. On Monday Bill Griffeth, the excellent anchor on CNBC, said he couldn't get the story about the Luby's chairman killing himself out of his head. Griffeth is usually so jocular and funny that we all stop and listen at my shop for his 1:55 PM droll lesson of the day. But that day he talked about how important it was to remember that even if business is going poorly, it's just business. It will come back. It will sort itself out. And if it doesn't, there will be another opportunity. But family, life — now that's real.

I picked up the phone and called my wife back. I said I am stopping the shoot right now no matter how much it costs, jumping into my car, and I will be there immediately.

Twenty minutes later I walked into the hospital and I could hear my daughter crying for her daddy all the way down the hall. I rushed in and she said, "Daddy, these people put this thing in my arm and it hurts, why didn't you stop them?" I explained to her that it was an IV, and she needed the energy from it. "But, Daddy," she asked, "Why didn't you get here sooner?"

I took a deep breath and said, "I got here as soon as I could." And for a moment, in all the turmoil, I felt good. I hadn't lied. I had gotten there as fast as I could.

Now it's 5:34 AM. My daughter slept well and is doing better already. I'm looking at my screens. I'll make it back. Things will be fine.

I did the right thing. Thanks, Bill.

James Cramer, CEO

TheStreet.com

What lies behind us and what lies before us are small matters compared to what lies within us.

Ralph Waldo Emerson

76

Two Doctors Not Chosen

Walking down the sidewalk, you're met by a well-dressed stranger who falls into step beside you. Gaining your attention, he extends his palm toward you and says, "I need only twenty dollars of your money." You are neither surprised nor offended. And of course it would be rude not to give him the money, so you quickly fork it over. You've gone less than a block when a woman steps in front of you, looks directly into your eyes, turns her palm upward, and says, "Fifteen dollars is all I need." Of course you give her the money because "that's what you're supposed to do," right?

Whether we give it away, lose it, squander it, or spend it wisely, when our money is gone, it's gone. But money is a renewable resource. Time, on the other hand, is not. We can "spend" the minutes and hours of our lives only once. So why are we more protective of our money than our time?

The average life expectancy is currently 75.7 years. This means that only 27,630 days will separate the doctor who slaps your butt from the one who pulls the sheet over your face. Assuming that you sleep 8 hours a night, you will have a total of 442,080 waking hours in those 75.7 years.

How will you spend those hours? What do you plan to buy with your life?

At a dollar an hour, your life is worth $442,080 dollars. Fifteen minutes is worth a quarter. At ten dollars an hour, those fifteen minutes are worth two-fifty. If your life is worth a hundred dollars an hour, fifteen minutes are worth twenty-five bucks. How much is your life worth? Are the minutes and hours of your life "owed" to everyone who knocks on your door, calls your telephone number, or asks you for an appointment? And how much TV do you really want to watch?

I'm fourteen years old. The telephone is ringing in the kitchen and I'm racing to answer it. Rounding the corner from the living room, I'm four steps away from the telephone . . . three steps . . . two steps. . . . Reaching out my hand, I hear the voice of my mother bark sharply, "Stop! Don't answer that." I turn and look at her in utter amazement. The telephone rings again. My face snaps instinctively toward it. I turn back to look at my mother. Her face is implacable. Again the telephone makes its demand. Rising from her seat at the kitchen table, Mom calmly walks over to stand beside me. Taking my hand in hers, she says, "We're just going to stand here together and watch it ring until it quits." I ask, "Mom, is there someone that you're avoiding?" She looks at me incredulously, "Of course not." That telephone rings on and on, begging me, pleading with me to answer it. Finally it goes silent. "In a home, one chooses to answer the telephone or not. There is no requirement that you do so. Any fool can dial our seven digits. That does not make them your master."

I never ran for the telephone again.

My mother used little moments like these to teach me that even though we were desperately poor and uneducated, we were still the masters of our own destiny, the controllers of our own lives.

Who is controlling yours?

Most of the critical things in life, which become the starting points of human destiny, are little things.

R. Smith

77

Have You Never
Been to Neverland?

I don't know whether you have ever seen a map of a person's mind. Doctors sometimes draw maps of other parts of you, and your own map can become intensely interesting, but catch them trying to draw a map of a child's mind, which is not only confused, but keeps going round all the time. There are zigzag lines on it, just like your temperature on a card, and these are probably roads in the island, for the Neverland is always more or less an island, with astonishing splashes of color here and there, and coral reefs and rakish-looking craft in the offing, and savages and lonely lairs, and gnomes who are mostly tailors, and caves through which a river runs, and princes with six elder brothers, and a hut fast going to decay, and one very small old lady with a hooked nose.

— J. M. Barrie, *Peter Pan*, chapter 1, paragraph 18

Sterling Randall Alexander Benningfield is celebrating the forty-sixth anniversary of his seventh birthday this year, and I've decided to help. Like all of Alex's birthday celebrations, this one is expected to last exactly 365 days. Then Alex will begin celebrating the forty-seventh anniversary of his seventh birthday. As you can see, Alex has been seven years old for a very long time.

In that tiny place where his world overlaps with mine, Alex is a self-made multimillionaire who owns a large corporation and is well known for his daring raids on Wall Street. But in the world where Alex lives alone, he is an adventurous pirate who wears an eye patch and a sword and keeps a knife firmly clenched between his teeth.

Following Alex through the strange oval door that leads into his private office, I notice that the opening is barely one inch higher than he is. Anyone who is taller than Alex must lower his head as he steps through the portal. Raising my head, I see that I'm now in the Captain's wood-planked cabin on an ancient sailing ship, where I'm surrounded by swords and maps and flintlock pistols and a real treasure chest that's overflowing with treasure. The Captain's desk and chair sit on a raised platform that's eight inches higher than the rest of the room.

"Alex," I ask, "do you have any idea how psychologically transparent all of this is?"

"Of course I do," he replies with a devilish grin as he steps up onto his elevated platform.

You've heard the story of a boy who lives in Neverland who claims that he will "never grow up." Most versions attribute that quote to Peter Pan, but they're wrong — it was Captain Hook. Grownups call him "that nut who flies the Jolly Roger from the flagpole above his mansion," but children just call him Alex. We're delighted to have been invited to his party.

My question for you today is this: Do you wish you knew Alex Benningfield, or are you glad you don't?

How long has it been since you visited Neverland?

All children, except one, grow up. They soon know that they will grow up, and the way Wendy knew was this. One day when she was two years old she was playing in a garden, and she plucked another flower and ran with it to her mother. I suppose she must have looked rather delightful, for Mrs. Darling put her hand to her heart and cried, "Oh, why can't you remain like this for ever!" This was all that passed between them on the subject, but henceforth Wendy knew that she must grow up. You always know after you are two. Two is the beginning of the end.

— J. M. Barrie, *Peter Pan*, chapter 1, paragraph 1 ॐ

78

Finegal or Abraham?

For the past several months, Florence Balcombe has been dating Finegal O'Flahertie, the baby boy of "Speranza," an unconventional poetess who fights for women's rights. To the outrage of many, the six-foot Speranza coolly justifies her public extravagances by saying that she is "above respectability."

Like his memorable mother, young Finegal is colorful and sensitive and writes poetry from the heart. But Florence Balcombe is the daughter of a lieutenant colonel who sees no great value in poetry or in the boys who write it. Lieutenant Colonel Balcombe much prefers young Abraham Stoker, a boy who had been sickly as a child but who "whipped himself into manhood" with a diet of strict discipline and athletic endurance. And like the lieutenant colonel, Abraham works as a civil servant. He is a file clerk at the courthouse.

In a single moment of pivotal decision, Florence rejects the marriage proposal of young Finegal O'Flahertie and chooses to become Mrs. Abraham Stoker instead. Brokenhearted, Finegal immediately flees to London and buries himself in his poetry. Later that year he wins the coveted Newdigate Prize for his poem "Ravenna," and it ignites in him a burning desire to achieve stardom. Since his mother has taught him to view everything in life as a performance, young Finegal is soon making a spectacle of everything, sometimes even hailing a cab just to cross the street. He has his clothes made by theater costumiers instead of tailors, since he feels they better understand the dramatic effect that he is trying to achieve. Soon Finegal O'Flahertie is the talk of all England.

Back home in Ireland, a slightly intimidated Abraham Stoker decides to publish a book of his own. Needless to say, *The Duties of*

Clerks of Petty Sessions in Ireland is not a huge success. In London, however, Finegal O'Flahertie continues to pile fame upon fame as both poet and playwright. His short stories and magazine articles are in constant demand.

When an old but powerful politician accuses Finegal of homosexuality, he quickly responds with a lawsuit. Interestingly, the politician, like Lieutenant Colonel Balcombe, is "a real man's man" who achieved his fame by writing the official rulebook for the sport of boxing.

Finegal loses the lawsuit. The macho politician then countersues, and on May 25, 1895, Oscar Finegal O'Flahertie Wills Wilde is sentenced to two years at hard labor for the crime of indecency.

Shortly after he is released from prison in 1897, Oscar learns that Florence's husband, 'Bram Stoker, has written another book. Within three years, that book, *Dracula*, has outsold every other book in history except the Bible.

On November 30, 1900, Oscar Finegal O'Flahertie Wills Wilde lay down and died in a rented room in Paris. He was forty-six years old. Doctors say that an infection of the inner ear was the likely culprit.

Those who knew him best did not agree. ༄

While still a young man, Oscar vowed, "I'll be a poet, a writer, a dramatist. Somehow or other I'll be famous, and if not famous I'll be notorious."

— *The Epigrams of Oscar Wilde*, 1952 Alvin Redman Ltd. London

79

Grit, Thy Name Is Andrew

A professional soldier understands that war means killing people, war means maiming people, war means families left without fathers and mothers. . . . Any soldier worth his salt should be antiwar. And still, there are things worth fighting for.

— Gen. H. Norman Schwarzkopf

Andrew marches cheerfully behind George Washington as they go to bravely fight the British. When it's discovered that the thirteen-year-old boy is an excellent rider, he's given the job of courier. But within a year he is captured and taken prisoner of war by the troops of Sir Banastre Tarleton, a British commander known throughout the Carolinas as "The Butcher."

As Andrew stands quietly at attention, Tarleton looks him over with a sneer. Lifting a muddy foot onto a wooden box in front of the lad, Tarleton says, "Boy, clean my boot." Andrew replies by suggesting that Tarleton do something quite different with "that boot." (Andrew's suggestion, by the way, is anatomically unfeasible.) A viper-quick blow from Tarleton's sword knocks Andrew off his feet and exposes the white bone of his forehead. Andrew is delirious for weeks and an invalid for months, but somehow he survives.

When the war is over, twenty-one-year-old Andrew moves to Nashville, where he rents a room from a Mrs. Donelson. He has been in her home only a few days when the door quietly opens and a young woman slips quickly inside, her wet cheeks bruised by the hand of a violent husband. Surprised by Andrew's presence, the girl quickly wipes the tears from her cheeks, composes herself, and politely asks, "Is my mother home? I'm Rachel Donelson Robards." Smitten, Andrew instantly becomes Rachel's guardian and protector. The two

are married three years later in the honest but mistaken belief that Rachel's husband, Lewis Robards, has obtained a legal divorce. They are stunned to hear, two years later, that Rachel's divorce has only just become final. They are immediately remarried in a second wedding ceremony.

Years later, when the famed duelist Charles Dickinson becomes furious at Andrew over a wager he has lost, he publicly accuses Rachel of having abandoned her husband to live in adultery with Andrew. Rachel, the love of Andrew's life, is devastated. Andrew immediately challenges Dickinson to a duel and tells a friend, "Though he shoot me in the brain, I will kill this man." The pistols are brought. The distance is stepped off. They face one another from twenty-four feet. Knowing Dickinson to be a faster and better shot, Andrew doesn't even try to shoot first, but calmly takes a bullet in the chest. It shatters two ribs and lodges near Andrew's heart. Then, without flinching, Andrew takes long and careful aim. Charles Dickinson dies on the spot.

Dickinson's bullet is still in Andrew's chest twenty-three years later, when he is inaugurated to serve as the seventh president of these United States.

Am I glorifying violence? Don't be silly. This story isn't about violence, but about tenacity, commitment, and resolve. Andrew Jackson knew what he was willing to die for. Right or wrong, his life revolved around his commitment to the creation of an American nation and his guardianship of Rachel Donelson. The only way to create a crisis in Andrew's life would have been to force him to choose between those two.

Is there anything that your life revolves around? If so, then your universe has a center, an anchor that gives you stability and lets you focus your energy, prioritize your time, and commit your heart. If your life has no such anchor, then you probably often feel as though you're floating aimlessly through time, drifting on the muddy, mindless tides of daily circumstance. Am I right? ❧

"The future doesn't belong to the fainthearted. It belongs to the brave."

— Ronald Reagan

80

Is Ours an "Any Road" Generation?

In 1967, Jefferson Airplane said, "Go ask Alice." So I did. Here's what I learned:

Abundant money and miraculous technologies confront us daily with an excess of options, while in the quiet shadows a debilitating apathy moans and whispers: "Nothing is special anymore."

You've heard these whisperings, haven't you?

I get the feeling these days that many people have no idea where they're going. Not in advertising. Not in business. Not in life. Stranger yet is the feeling that they just don't care. Back in 1865, when Lewis Carroll's Cheshire Cat first quipped, "If you don't care very much where you are going, any road will get you there," the comment was considered comically absurd.

It's not so funny anymore.

Are we becoming an Any Road generation?

Faith Popcorn warned us about the insidious danger of too many choices back in 1991, when she wrote, "We used to believe that we could become anything we wanted to be. But now we tell ourselves that we can be everything we want to be." Pennie agrees with Faith's statement and says, "Most people are reluctant to choose, because they don't want to leave anything out." But she also notes a second, more perplexing problem. "Others are afraid to choose because they fear they'll make the wrong choice."

Hmm. . . . Afraid to choose. Let's talk about that:

1. Most choices are less important than the fact that you made a choice. So make one. Do it. Provide yourself with a direction. By choosing a destination, you give yourself hope and a plan.

2. Never look back at "what might have been." If you spend too much time looking in life's rear-view mirror, you're going to have a horrible crash. It's the surest way to become an emotional cripple.

3. In the end, it isn't important whether you ever arrive at your destination. What matters most is that you had a purpose, a personal code of conduct, and a beautiful dream.

"A personal code of conduct?"

Question: Is your behavior the result of your genetic makeup, or are you merely a product of your environment? This weary debate is commonly referred to as "Nature vs. Nurture," and it's an old and foolish argument. The Nature people say, "You can't help it. You just inherited a bad chromosome." The Nurture people say, "You can't help it. It's just how you were raised." I say, "Piffle and pooh, you CAN help it. You're going to choose what you will do."

The point I'm trying to make is this: You are much more than the random product of a genetic lottery, and you are much bigger than your environment. You, my friend, are becoming, with every passing moment, the product of your choices.

So what will you choose?

Indecision is debilitating. If feeds upon itself; it is, one might almost say, habit-forming. Not only that, but it is contagious; it transmits itself to others. . . . Business is dependent upon action. It cannot go forward by hesitation. Those in executive positions must fortify themselves with facts and accept responsibility for decisions based upon them. Often greater risk is involved in postponement than making a wrong decision.

Harry A. Hopf

81

Pull the Trigger and Ride the Bullet

How far would Moses have gone if he had taken a poll in Egypt?
What would Jesus Christ have preached if he had taken a poll in
the land of Israel? What would have happened to the Reformation
if Martin Luther had taken a poll? It isn't polls or public opinion of
the moment that counts. It's right and wrong and leadership.

— Harry S Truman

My best friend, Tony, is a deep recluse. Such a recluse,
in fact, that no one in recent years has been able to
completely confirm his existence. I'm not even sure
Tony has a social security number; I know that he's
certainly never had a regular job. My staff thinks Tony is just a figment
of my imagination. But he's not.

When we were in high school, Tony bought and sold cars on the
weekends. I watched with interest as he made and lost thousands of
dollars. Later, I watched Tony become the owner of a small oil
company and then a wholesaler of fine furniture.

I comforted Tony the day his first wife ran off with the carnival,
and I was there when he learned the state had auctioned off his "free
and clear" house for back taxes. I answered the phone when he called
for me to bail him out of jail after he'd held a gun to the head of his
first wife's boyfriend. Recently, I watched as Tony sold the wrong
stock short in a day trade and was forced to cough up a quarter
million dollars.

I've watched my friend Tony do some extraordinarily stupid things
over the past twenty-five years, but not once have I ever heard him
whine about how things turned out. For all his faults, Tony takes
complete and utter responsibility. I've never seen him point a finger
toward anyone but himself. When most people would be wailing,

"Oh God, why me?" Tony simply looks up to the heavens, shrugs his shoulders, and says, "I pulled the trigger and rode the bullet."

Are you able to make a decision and then live with the consequences? Do you have the courage of your convictions, or do you find yourself vacillating, waffling, and wringing your hands whenever you must make an important decision? I've learned a valuable lesson from my friend Tony, and you'd do well to learn it, too: Whenever there is a decision to be made, make it! Don't be a hand-wringing weasel.

Every tomorrow is shaped by the choices of today. You know this, and it scares you, right? Quit worrying! While tomorrow will be shaped by today's choices, the day after tomorrow will be shaped by tomorrow's choices. Each and every day of your life, you get one more chance to get it right.

Later today you'll be faced with a choice and will have to make an important decision. In that moment, I hope you'll examine your options and then do what must be done. No hand-wringing. No moaning. No hopping back and forth from one foot to the other.

Just make a decision and live with it. Pull the trigger and ride the bullet. ❧

82

A Classic Shagger

"What am I bid for this classic Shagger?" I'm sitting in the third row at the famous James C. Leake auction in Tulsa watching a tuxedoed British auctioneer work a roomful of Oklahoma oilmen. Ninety seconds later, the auctioneer drops his hammer and the Shagger sells for a record price. Just then, Tony leans over, cups his hand to my ear and whispers, "I've got a car just like that at home, but mine's called a JAG-wire and it won't bring anywhere near that kind of money."

Sometimes the power of a thing isn't in the thing itself but in the way you present it. There are no rules to the game called "Style"; it's a game that anyone with enough boldness and audacity can win.

No one knows this better than Gabrielle.

Gabrielle is a little orphan girl who lives with her two aunts in a desolate section of rural France. In 1899, at age sixteen, Gabrielle runs off with Etienne Balsan, a young cavalry officer who calls her "Little Pet," the name by which she will become known throughout the world.

At age thirty, Little Pet opens a boutique in Paris where she breaks every rule of fashion. Occasionally her rule-breaking is based purely on practicality: she wears bell-bottom trousers in Venice only because she feels it will be easier to climb in and out of gondolas in them. It starts a pants revolution. After accidentally singeing her hair, she decides to cut it off completely and boldly strolls into the Paris Opera that way. It starts a craze for bobbed hair. While watching a boyfriend play polo, she becomes chilled and borrows his blazer. It turns so many heads that she immediately begins designing what will become known as her famous "box jacket."

Throughout her life of eighty-seven years, Little Pet is bold, driven, and intense. "There is time for work. And time for love," she says. "That leaves no other time." Little Pet's friends include Picasso, Churchill, Dali, Cocteau, Stravinsky, and Princess Grace. Her Paris boutique will have more than 3,500 employees and her designer perfume will become the most famous in the world. In the movie about her life, Katherine Hepburn will be chosen to play the lead. When she passes away in 1971, *TIME* magazine calls her "the 20th century's single most important arbiter of fashion."

How does she do it? What secret energy does Little Pet use to rocket herself from the desolate fields of rural France onto the covers of every fashion magazine in the world? The answer, in a word, is generosity. Throughout her life, Little Pet never once tried to "protect" her style. Anyone who wanted to sell knockoffs of her products was perfectly welcome to do so. Little Pet knew that it would only make her more famous.

When one of the world's wealthiest men, the Duke of Westminster, asked her to marry him, she turned him down flatly, saying, "There are a lot of duchesses, but only one Coco* Chanel."

You go, girl.

* "Coco" is French for "little pet."

We make way for the man who boldly pushes past us.

Christian Bovee

185

83

The Rainbow and the Woodster

I always assumed until recently that rainbows disappeared from sight long before they touched the earth and that searching for the end of the rainbow was nothing more than a game for the gullible. Or that, if rainbows did touch the earth, they moved with the viewer, so that you could spend all day chasing one and never be closer than you were when you started.

But now I know the truth: rainbows do reach the ground and you can walk into them and through them and be wrapped in luminous ribbons of color. I know this is true because I've done it.

The rainbow was a big one, making landfall in the center of a new-mown lawn at the southeast corner of Koenig and Lamar in Austin. Pennie, Rex, and Jake were all with me, as well as Woody Justice, the original client of my firm and a very dear friend. (Not many years ago, back in the days when Woody and I were both desperately poor, I made a solemn pledge to him that I would do everything in my power to help him succeed, and he pledged the same to me. For my part, I began telling Springfield, Missouri what a wonderful jeweler Woody was. For his part, the Woodster began telling the world that I was the Wizard of Ads.)

Now back to the corner of Koenig and Lamar. Standing and staring at the end of a rainbow that was physically touching the earth less than 100 feet in front of me, I now had a new question: Where was my leprechaun with his pot of gold?

Having had a few months to think about it, I've concluded that there can only be three possible answers:

1. There is no pot of gold at the end of a rainbow.
2. Someone else had gotten there first and taken it.

3. The leprechaun was riding in the car with me and had already given me his pot of gold.

(If you'll examine the picture of Woody Justice on page 31 of my first book, *The Wizard of Ads,* I think you'll agree that possibility number three is not only possible but more than a little likely.)

How about you? Do you have a friend who works day and night to help you reach your goals? Is there a person in your life who always cheers you on, no matter what? If so, I think that perhaps you, too, have touched the colors at the end of the rainbow.

Accept the things to which fate binds you, and love the people with whom fate brings you together, but do so with all your heart.

Marcus Aurelius

Wyoming rainbow.

84

What Was I Thinking?

"Band-Aid Beige" is the only way to describe the color of the car I just bought. My friend Tony calls it "Caucasian." Either way, I'm pretty sure it's the only Corvette in the world ever to be painted this color.

Tony and I suspect that some guy in a paint booth at General Motors was bored out of his wits one afternoon and said, "I think I'll paint the next Corvette beige, just to see what it looks like." When he saw the car in the drying room later that afternoon, he muttered to himself, "Good God, what was I thinking?" and quickly wrote someone else's name on the paint job's completion slip.

Ever since I bought the car, that painter's mumbled question has been running through my own mind as well: "Good God, what was I thinking?"

Our younger son, Jake, took one look at the car, turned to me, and said, "Dad, you're not gonna become one of those old guys who unbuttons his shirt down to his navel and starts wearing a lot of gold jewelry, are you?" Before I could answer him, his brother Rex began swiveling his hips in his best "groovy dude" imitation and said, "Ohhhh yeahhh, baby, he's a real 'smack-daddy' now." Pennie quickly turned her head so that I wouldn't see her smile.

What was I thinking?

I was thinking of the day when my mother, thirty-two years old and divorced from a sixteen-year marriage, announced that she was going to buy herself "a Corvette car" as soon as she could afford one. I was eleven when she said it and thought, "I have the coolest mom on earth."

I was thinking of the Saturday morning, nine years later, when Tony and I went with her to help pick out a used Corvette. Tony is an automotive genius who, by the age of nineteen, had already bought and sold more than 100 cars. "Is this car mechanically sound?" asked my Mom. "Yeah, it's plenty tight," said Tony, "but when it comes to resale, that color. . . ." "I'll take it," Mom told the owner. "I've never seen another one like it."

So why did the world's coolest mom decide to sell her signature Corvette after twenty years? Was it because she's now a silver-haired retiree and considered it no longer appropriate? No, the reason she sold it was because she couldn't fit it into a suitcase. Mom recently packed two small overnight bags with her most comfortable clothes and then sold all her remaining earthly possessions and moved to the Costa del Sol in Spain. In her most recent letter to us, she says her apartment overlooks the sun-drenched Mediterranean. Mom doesn't speak a word of Spanish, German, Italian, or French, but says that she intends to learn. Her plan is to spend the balance of her years exploring all the nooks and crannies of Europe.

So why does a sixty-two-year-old woman sell everything she owns and move to Europe? Because it's something she had always wanted to do, and unlike most of us, she actually had the guts to do it.

Is there anything you've always wanted to do?

They're a right sorry admission of defeat, them signs are. If my life was that compromised, I sure wouldn't advertise it. My sign would say, "If There Was Something Else I'd Rather Be Doing, I'd Damn Well Be Doing It."

Tom Robbins, *Skinny Legs and All* (Boomer Petway)

85

Nathan's Little Flags

Twice each day, Mocatta, Pixley, Montagu, Nathan, and "Yankee" meet at Nathan's place on St. Swithin's Lane in London. During these meetings, each of them will raise and lower little Union Jack flags until the glorious moment arrives when all five flags are down simultaneously. It is at precisely that moment that five obscure individuals, Mocatta, Pixley, Montagu, Nathan, and "Yankee," will have established the worldwide price of gold.

The story begins with a man named Amschel, an insignificant collector of old coins who lived in the ghettos of Frankfurt, Germany during the late 1700s. Due to his specialized knowledge of coins, Amschel soon became the official "seeker of old coins" for a wealthy and powerful coin collector, the Landgrave William IX of Hesse-Kassel.

In 1805, impressed with the financial insight of Amschel's twenty-eight-year-old son, Nathan, William IX entrusts a large portion of his wealth to him and asks that Nathan invest it for him. But rather than buying and selling old coins as his father had done, Nathan chooses to buy and sell gold bullion. One day Nathan reports, "I know of only two men who really understand the true value of gold — an obscure clerk in the basement vault of the Banque de Paris, and one of the directors of the Bank of England. And unfortunately, they disagree! But don't worry, sir, I have a plan."

Soon Nathan is receiving advance information through a series of carefully arranged flag signals from France across the English Channel. Since Nathan is receiving his information much faster than the other traders, he quickly amasses a staggering fortune. Seventeen years later, Francis I of Austria makes Nathan a baron.

And that, in a nutshell, is why a representative from the Mocatta Group (a division of Standard Chartered Bank), Deutsche Bank Sharps Pixley, Montagu Precious Metals (part of Hong Kong Shanghai Banking Corp.), and Republic National Bank of New York (The Yankee Bank) meet twice each day to raise and lower little flags as they fix the worldwide price of gold. And at whose place do they meet on St. Swithin's Lane in London? Why, the headquarters of the Baron Nathan Mayer de Rothschild, of course.

And that's how the worldwide price of gold is established by five obscure individuals in London at 10:30 each morning and at 3:00 each afternoon, to this very day.

The beginnings of all things are small.

Cicero

86

Extreme Accidental Magic

The Associated Press may own the copyright, but I own the actual photograph. I'm not really sure why I bought it, though. You can't even see the faces of the six people in it. I'm told their names were Ira, Mike, Franklin, Harlon, Rene, and John, but that's not really important. Ultimately, it's just a photograph of six people doing something that people do every day.

But for them to do it that day was crazy. The photographer who took the photo was crazy, and I was crazy to buy it. I do crazy things sometimes. I'll bet you do, too. And like me, you probably have no better explanation than "It seemed like the right thing to do at the time." Fortunately, Pennie tolerates my irresponsible behavior. Maybe she even loves me for it. That's one of the many advantages of marrying your best friend.

But I really do like this photo. It's special, somehow. Beyond the fact that three of the six people in it died shortly after the photographer's shutter went "click," the photo is unique because everything about it was an accident and Accidental Magic is the theme of my collection. This particular accident happened when a photographer named Joe Rosenthal heard a noise and, swinging his camera toward it, pressed his finger on the camera's shutter and captured a millisecond of history by accident. The millisecond happened on February 23, 1945. The photo is called "Raising the Flag Over Iwo Jima."

I bought the photo, through a broker, from the estate of John Faber, the man who became the official historian for the National Press Photographers Association in 1956. Faber kept the job and the photograph until the day he died. Faber had obtained the photo from Joe Rosenthal, the Associated Press photographer who had actually snapped it. In the preface of his 1977 book, *Great News Photos and the Stories Behind Them*, Faber writes, "Assembling this book has been a series of unforgettable experiences for me. I listened again to my tape recording of Joe Rosenthal describing, in his humble way, the day he made the Iwo Jima Flag Raising picture. . . ."

Gosh, I wish I could find that tape.

I really do hope that you'll come to visit us sometime and take a long, hard look at this picture. It's a photo that speaks of all the best in us — heroism, sacrifice, principles, and honor. But it also speaks of the worst — anger, violence, killing, and war. Yes, there are two ways of looking at this photo. There are two ways of looking at everything. Wisdom is often found in the ability to look at a thing from both sides and not feel you have to choose between them. It is perhaps that very tension that makes the photo a profound and powerful millisecond of history.

In his book *Flags of Our Fathers*, James Bradley opens with a quote from a Japanese man, Yoshikani Taki, who said, "Mothers should negotiate between nations. The mothers of the fighting countries would agree: Stop this killing now. Stop it now." What makes James Bradley's use of this quote particularly interesting is that the man in the center of the Iwo Jima photograph was James Bradley's father, John, and it was the ancestors of Yoshikani Taki whom John Bradley had been sent to Iwo Jima to kill.

Our spinning world is an interesting place, but you've got to hang on tight. ❧

What helps luck is a habit of watching for opportunities, of having a patient, but restless mind, of sacrificing one's ease or vanity, or uniting a love of detail to foresight, and of passing through hard times bravely and cheerfully.

Charles Victor Cherbuliez

87

The Value of Heroes

The saying "The sun never sets on the British Empire" was true as recently as 1937 when tiny England did, in fact, still have possessions in each of the world's twenty-four time zones. It's widely known that the British explored, conquered, and ruled much of the world for a number of years, but what isn't as widely known is what made them believe they could do it.

See a 1937 map of British possessions in the world's 24 time zones at www.friesian.com/british.htm

For the first 1,000 years after Christ, Greece and Rome were the only nations telling stories of heroes and champions. England was just a dreary little island of rejects, castoffs, barbarians, and losers. So who inspired tiny, foggy England to rise up and take over the world?

Hoping to instill in his countrymen a sense of pride, a simple Welsh monk named Geoffrey assembled a complete history of England that gave his people a grand and glorious pedigree. Published in 1136, Geoffrey's *History of the Kings of Britain* was a detailed written account of the deeds of the English people for each of the seventeen centuries prior to AD 689 . . . and not a single word of it was true. Yet in creating Merlyn, Guinevere, Arthur, and the Knights of the Round Table from the fabric of imagination, Geoffrey of Monmouth persuaded a sad little island of rejects, castoffs, barbarians, and losers to see themselves as a just and magnificent nation.

Did you, like most people, think that Thomas Malory's *Le Morte D'Arthur* was the origin of Arthurian legend? Nope, Malory's work, published in 1485, was based on Geoffrey's "history," which had been published and widely circulated 349 years earlier.

And not long after they began to see themselves that way in their minds, they began seeing themselves that way in the mirror.

Most people assume that legends, myths, and stories of heroes are simply the byproducts of great civilizations, but I'm convinced that they are the cause of them. Throughout history, the mightiest civilizations have been the ones with stories of heroes, larger-than-life role models who inspired ordinary citizens to rise up and do amazing things.

It's no secret that people will usually do in reality what they have seen themselves do in their minds.

In your mind, what do you see yourself doing?

Heroes are created by popular demand, sometimes out of the scantiest materials.

Gerald W. Johnson

88

Weiners, Beans, and $530 Million

Evan Chrapko and his brother, Shane, sold their two-year-old Internet business for more than half a billion dollars.

Unless I miss my guess, right now you're probably thinking, "So two guys made a lot of money on an Internet startup. Big deal. Lots of Internet techies cashed in for big bucks in the late 1990s. My only problem is that I wasn't an Internet techie."

Oddly enough, neither were Evan and Shane Chrapko. "Well, it takes money to make money, so Evan and Shane obviously come from a wealthy family, right?" No, Evan and Shane were raised on the Chrapko family farm in rural Alberta, Canada. On the day their multimillionaire status was announced, their father, Victor, found it difficult to grasp the financial success of his sons. He said, "Before I see it in their bank account, I don't believe it."

But it is to this same man that the boys give all the credit for their success. Wearing a black knit shirt, faded jeans, and a felt cowboy hat, Evan says, "Growing up on the farm together prepared us well for doing business together." Nodding in agreement, Shane adds, "Mom and Dad taught us the importance of being calm under pressure and seeing two sides to every issue." During the years that they were developing their company, DocSpace, Evan and Shane slept at the office each night and lived on a diet of wieners and beans.

No, Evan and Shane Chrapko aren't a couple of young technical geniuses. Evan brought into the business a degree in accounting, and Shane contributed his years of experience as a river-rafting tour guide. People who know them best characterize their greatest assets as being (1) the deep trust they have in their friends and in each other, (2) their passion for an idea, and (3) their willingness to follow through on a plan, regardless of the barriers.

An interesting story, right? Let me tell you how it ends: Ten years from now, Evan and Shane will look back on their days of wieners and beans as being the happiest days of their lives. I guarantee this unconditionally. Their single biggest worry will be how to give their children the hardships that made them rich. Their second biggest worry will be the motives of all the people who want to be their friends.

Are you still in the wieners-and-beans stage of your life? If so, let me encourage you to celebrate each and every day. Rich folks don't get to experience the joys of anticipation like you do, and there are no better friends in the world than those who will eat wieners and beans with you. Why not get 'em all together and tell 'em how much they mean to you? After they've had their laughs and ridiculed you for being a sloppy, sentimental fool, you can sit around together and feast a great feast upon the very finest wieners and beans. Twenty-five years from now, these moments will be your fondest memories.

This, too, I guarantee unconditionally. ❧

In prosperity it is very easy to find a friend;
in adversity, nothing is so difficult.

Epictetus

89

Griswold's Billion-Dollar Prank

The young do not know enough to be prudent, and therefore they attempt the impossible — and achieve it, generation after generation.

— Pearl S. Buck

You are Pierre Lorillard IV, heir to a vast tobacco fortune. As a Lorillard, you move in the highest social circles and are considered to be a pillar of New York's Fifth Avenue society, even though you live forty miles north of Manhattan.

As you stroll the sidewalks of New York City this fine autumn day, you look toward the harbor and see a mountain of unsightly crates that are said to hold a gigantic statue of a woman holding a torch and wearing a crown. There has been quite a local ruckus about whether to assemble the statue or ship it back to the French. You vote for shipping it back. Your son, Griswold, however, thinks it should be installed on an island in the harbor where it can greet the incoming immigrants. Young men can be so impulsive. You turn and wave to the Roosevelts, making direct eye contact with "Teddy," the one they say has political aspirations. Perhaps it will someday prove helpful to know him.

Your principal concern at the moment, however, is that it's time once again for the Autumn Ball in the small community where you live. You were hoping to wear something a little less formal than the short, black jacket with the extremely long, split tails that has become the standard of men's formal wear. At your request, a Manhattan tailor has designed several new, black formal jackets, and you're on your way to look at them.

Arriving at the tailor's shop to examine the jackets, you are instantly chagrined, wondering if perhaps a friend has bribed the tailor to play an elaborate joke on you. Though you are more than a little angry, you smile sweetly as you gently decline to pay for the jackets, saying only, "No, I fear these simply won't do at all." You then walk unceremoniously out of his shop, thinking, "Let him eat those jackets for his supper. No tailor will make a fool out of me."

Later that evening, you are stunned as your son, Griswold, swaggers into the party with his friends. They're all wearing the black jackets that you, earlier that very afternoon, declined! You listen with rising horror as murmurs ripple across the room: "But those jackets are shaped exactly like the bright red jackets the English wear when they're out hunting foxes!" To make matters worse, Griswold and his friends are wearing red vests beneath the tailless, black riding coats. Throughout the evening, the boys smile broadly and say, "Yes, we're hunting foxes," as they glance at the young ladies about the room. You leave the Autumn Ball early, certain that you will never live down the shame of this night. A few days later, you are relieved to learn that the boys' lofty charm and social status has resulted in their outfits being imitated rather than condemned.

"Youth is the opportunity to do something and to become somebody."
— Theodore T. Munger

Today, the sale and rental of those jackets brings in more than half a billion dollars a year in the United States alone. It's impossible to imagine a wedding or a high school prom without them. And we owe it all to a silly prank played in 1886 by Griswold Lorillard and his pals on the evening of the Autumn Ball in a little community north of New York City known as Tuxedo Park. ❧

Life is at its best when it's shaken and stirred.

F. Paul Facault

90

Martin's Very Big Day

His name was Martin, and in the early 1500s he wrote a thing that changed our world forever. As Martin dipped pen in ink that momentous day, he could not possibly have known the degree to which he was redefining our future. No, Martin innocently put pen to paper and forever changed our world, never once suspecting the full magnitude of what he was doing.

If you assume that I'm referring to the day in 1517 when a man named Martin Luther ignited the flames of the Protestant Reformation, well, you're wrong. The Martin of whom I write was very near the end of his life on the day that Martin Luther nailed his Ninety-Five Theses to the door of the Wittenberg Castle church. The Martin of whom I speak had done his scribbling exactly ten years, six months, and six days earlier. It was on April 25, 1507, that Martin Waldseemüller scribbled the word "America" on the map of a continent that had previously had no name. Martin, you see, was a mapmaker.

Martin's Universalis Cosmographia was the first map to show the New World as being composed of two continents joined by a narrow strait. The southern landmass, previously known as the "Western Indies," Martin designated "America." In *Cosmographiae Introductio,* the book that accompanied the map, Martin explained that he had named the New World after Amerigo Vespucci, the man who he believed had discovered it. Nine years later, Martin acknowledged Columbus as the true discoverer and immediately dropped the name "America" from his maps. But by then it was too late. America was here to stay.

Martin's decision in 1507, however, was of far less impact than many of the decisions you and I make each day. Martin's decision affected only the name of a country, a word on a map. Our decisions affect the lives of human beings. We choose to encourage someone and, in so doing, help shape his future success. We repeat gossip and, in so doing, create a breach that may never be healed. We contribute our time or money and, in so doing, make the world just a little bit better.

Today we will choose whether to frown or to smile. We will choose whether to hide love or show it. We will, by our choices, encourage or discourage the people around us. And each of these choices will have a far greater impact on the future of our world than did the meaningless markings of a mistaken mapmaker named Martin.

What kind of future will you choose? ❧

My own view of history is that human beings do have genuine freedom to make choices. Our destiny is not predetermined for us; we determine it for ourselves.

Arnold Toynbee

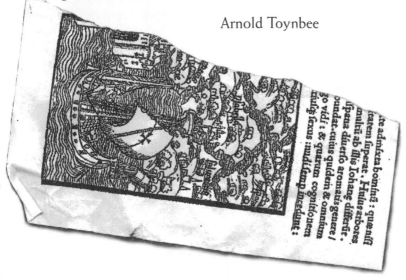

91

Curiosity and a Cat Named Adrian

Curiosity killed the cat" is an expression often quoted by the terminally dull, but I've never been able to make any sense of the statement. To which cat does this old adage refer? I'm aware of no story, myth, fable, or fairy tale in which a cat dies of curiosity.

But I do know a story about a contemporary Englishman named Adrian.

Adrian Nicholas was curious about a small sketch drawn by Leonardo da Vinci in the margin of a notebook nearly 500 years ago. Beneath this obscure and unremarkable sketch, Leonardo had added these few words: "If a man is provided with a length of gummed linen cloth with a length of 12 yards on each side and 12 yards high, he can jump from any great height whatsoever without injury." Modern experts have long been united in their agreement that Leonardo da Vinci was wrong. Very wrong.

Adrian Nicholas, however, wasn't so sure. Using only the tools and materials that would have been available to Leonardo in 1514, Adrian Nicholas built Leonardo's 187-pound, pyramid-shaped, canvas and wood contraption, and on June 27, 2000, took it with him in a hot-air balloon to an altitude of 10,000 feet, and then cheerfully jumped out with it.

You gotta love a guy like that.

Even though it's been more than sixty weeks since Adrian jumped, I figure Leonardo is still struttin' around the streets of heaven, high-fiving all his buddies and saying, "That's right. Uh-huh. I'm bad. I'm bad. You know I'm bad," because from the majestic skies above Mpumalanga, South Africa, Adrian Nicholas lazily floated to perfect safety beneath Leonardo's canvas pyramid, saying the ride was "smoother than with modern parachutes." Heathcliff O'Malley, who photographed Adrian's drop from a helicopter, said, "It was amazing, really beautiful. But none of us knew if it would fold up and Adrian would plummet to earth. . . . It works, and everyone thought it wouldn't."

Like Leonardo da Vinci, Adrian Nicholas is a curious person. As were Queen Isabella of Spain, Claude Monet of France, and Benjamin Franklin of the Red, White, and Blue. Are you a curious person?

One of the many benefits of curiosity is that curious people are seldom bored.

Conversely, boring people are seldom curious.

Which are you?

Curiosity is one of the most permanent and certain characteristics of a vigorous intellect.

Samuel Johnson

92

The Loneliest Man

Excruciatingly shy, Charles Lutwidge Dodgson lived a lonely childhood. Bullied and tormented by the older children because of his severe stammering, Charlie turned ten on January 27, 1842, and he remained ten years old until the day he died in 1898. Though he lived to be nearly sixty-seven, Charlie never overcame his stuttering problem, except, curiously, in the presence of little girls younger than eleven. He was to them a brilliant entertainer and a friend, their knight in shining armor.

Charlie was fascinated with inversions. His favorite game was to change one letter of a word to make an entirely new word, and to continue doing so until he had created a word that was related to the original, such as changing "WHEAT" to "BREAD," then "BREAD" to "TOAST":

WHEAT ➤ CHEAT ➤ CHEAP ➤ CHEEP ➤ CREEP ➤ CREED ➤ BREED ➤
BREAD ➤ BREAK ➤ BLEAK ➤ BLEAT ➤ BLEST ➤ BLAST ➤ BOAST ➤ TOAST

(Sound easy? Then why not try a simple one, like changing "HEAD" to "FOOT," "SLEEP" to "DREAM," or "LINEN" to "SHEET"? Charlie accomplished each of these and hundreds of others as well!) ✱

Though painfully shy, Charlie was highly organized, keeping a register of every letter he ever wrote. Upon his death, Charlie's register filled twenty-four volumes and listed 98,721 letters.

Perhaps the loneliest man who ever lived, Charlie had insomnia, ate only one meal a day, and never married. His only joy was playing games with little kids.

Henry Liddell, dean of Christ Church College, employed Charlie as a logician and a professor of mathematics, posts he held at the college until the end of his life. On July 4, 1862, Henry Liddell asked Charlie if he would row his three daughters up the Thames

*For the solutions to the doublets, visit thinks.com/puzzles/doublets.htm

River from Oxford to Godstow for a picnic and then row them back home before dark. Delighted, Charlie spent the entire day telling the girls a fantastic story in which Liddell's nine-year-old daughter was the heroine. Upon returning home, the little girl begged Charlie to "please write the story down." A few days later, Charlie presented her mother with a lengthy, hand-written account and assumed he had heard the last of it.

Not long after, novelist Henry Kingsley visited the deanery and happened to pick up the story from the drawing room table. Reading it, he urged Mrs. Liddell to persuade the author to publish it. The daughter's name, by the way, was Alice, and Charlie's story was about her adventures in a place of inverted reality called "Wonderland." True to his love for inversions, the book was published only after Charlie inverted his Christian name to Lutwidge Charles, then translated it to the Latin, Ludovicius Carolus, from which he then anglicized it to Lewis Carroll. Though he, himself, could never speak clearly, the names and sayings of his characters — the March Hare, the Mad Hatter, the Cheshire Cat, and the White Knight — have become part of our everyday speech. Only the Bible and Shakespeare are quoted more often. ❧

93

Moon River

Remember Andy Williams, the silver-voiced crooner who had his own TV show back in the 1960s? How about Alice Cooper, the first of the gory '70s shock-rockers? Now imagine a happy quartet composed of Andy Williams, Alice Cooper, 1940s sing-along cowboy Gene Autry, and adult magazine publisher Hugh Hefner. Sounds unlikely at best, right?

Well, it happened.

Although the philosophical and stylistic differences separating these men were definitely "wider than a mile," the four unlikely comrades did, in fact, come together to save a sentimental icon that was very dear to each of them. Williams, Cooper, Autry, and Hefner joined hands, hearts, and wallets to refurbish a decrepit, five-story billboard in Los Angeles. What was it that made the sign so special to Andy, Alice, Gene, and Hugh? Perhaps it had to do with the fact that, like each one of them, the sign was glitzy, larger than life, and completely homemade.

Built in 1923 to promote a Beachwood Canyon subdivision, the strange, homemade sign became the property of the city in 1944, when the company that had erected it filed bankruptcy. Not wanting to draw attention to a failed area subdivision, the city of Los Angeles chopped off a third of the sign's message, hoping that newcomers would now assume it was simply a navigational landmark.

It worked. Once the last four letters, L-A-N-D, were removed, hundreds of thousands of dreamers, hopefuls, cornballs, and crazies, including Andy Williams, Alice Cooper, Gene Autry, and Hugh Hefner, were brightly encouraged each day as they drove past Mount Lee in Griffith Park. No longer did they see a tacky, promotional billboard for Hollywoodland, the failed subdivision of 1923; they saw instead a glitzy, larger-than-life landmark of nine white letters sprawled across a mountainside that somehow seemed to whisper to them, "Never give up. Never give in. This is the place where dreams come true."

So now you know.

L.A. is a great big freeway.
Put a hundred down and buy a car.
In a week, maybe two, they'll make you a star.
Weeks turn into years. How quick they pass.
And all the stars that never were
Are parking cars and pumping gas.

— From "Do You Know the Way to San Jose?"
by Hal David and Burt Bacharach
Immortalized by Dionne Warwick

94

How 'Bout Those Canadians, Eh?

I wear a little Canadian flag on my lapel these days as a statement of my admiration for the people of Canada. Having made several trips there recently, I think I've finally figured out what it is that makes Canadians a little different from you and me. In a word or two, it's the Canadian Perspective.

Canadians look at things differently from those of us who live in these frantic United States. And when it comes to happiness and contentment, seeing things differently offers real advantages. For one, it's the root of all laughter. Were you aware that many of America's greatest comedians and comic actors are actually Canadian? Jim Carrey, Mike Myers, Dan Aykroyd, John Candy, Norm MacDonald, Michael J. Fox, David Foley, Mathew Perry, Howie Mandel, Rick Moranis, Martin Short. Canadians, every one. Likewise the great Thomas Chong of Cheech and Chong and the late Phil Hartman of *NewsRadio* and *Saturday Night Live.* Canadians, both. (Speaking of *Saturday Night Live,* you know Lorne Michaels, the writer and producer of that show? Yep, he's another one.)

You know that Canada is exactly like the U.S., except that it's cleaner and has friendlier people and a lot less crime, right? Each of these differences can be directly attributed to the Canadian Perspective, which, in a nutshell, is this: Canadians care. They genuinely, truly, and honestly care. (Don't ask me why they care or how they learned to care. I really don't know. My best guess is that the cold Canadian winters made them huddle up and get to know each other, and after they got to know one another, they said, "Hey, you're not so bad. . . .")

Trust me, one can learn a lot from a trip to Canada. (Uh-oh. I can already hear the rednecks bellowing, "I don't believe in travelin' outside the U.S. when there's plenty to see right here in 'merica. . . .") But I'm not suggesting that you travel to see mountains, canyons, lakes, rivers, or buildings. I'm suggesting that you travel to meet people who are different from you. It's worth a trip to Canada just to talk to a Canadian cop. His warm attitude and big grin will remind you so much of Andy Griffith that you'll think you're in Mayberry.

Do you resent me saying that Canadians, as a rule, seem to care more than we do? Have I made you angry by implying that we could learn a thing or two from our brothers and sisters to the North? Does it make you uncomfortable that Canadians might actually be better than us at more than just ice hockey?

Canadians have figured out that caring about people doesn't cause the same kind of stress as caring about things. Canadians are more concerned with who they are being than with what they are doing.

All in all, it's not a bad way to live, eh?

Travel is fatal to prejudice, bigotry, and narrow-mindedness.

Mark Twain

95

American Indian Eloquence

America's Thanksgiving holiday originated when the Pilgrims gave thanks to God for sending them an Indian friend named Squanto. This much you already knew. What you didn't know is that long before the Pilgrims landed at Plymouth Rock, this same Squanto had been captured by two English sea captains, George Weymouth and John Hunt, and abused as a slave for fourteen years. Squanto had been free less than five years when Capt. John Bradford's Pilgrims arrived on the good ship *Mayflower*.

Squanto had every reason to organize a killing party and wipe out the pale-skinned invaders, but he chose to help them instead. Gazing with pity at Bradford's pathetic band of would-be settlers as they huddled around Plymouth Rock, Squanto thought, "If I don't help these silly white men, they're all going to die in the coming winter." And with that, he walked out of the woods and introduced himself.

Squanto died two years later of a disease contracted from these same Europeans.

When I was a boy, all the movies were about heroic cowboys and evil Indians. And in virtually every one of them, courageous settlers had to circle the wagons to defend themselves against unprovoked attacks from apelike Indians who said things like, "Ugh. Me wantum whiskey."

Would you like to know how Indians actually spoke back then? Consider the musings of Ispwo Mukika Crowfoot, a Blackfoot Indian who was twenty years old in 1803, the year Lewis and Clark launched their famous expedition. As he lay dying, Ispwo left us with these last words: "What is life? It is the flash of a firefly in the night. It is the breath of a buffalo in the wintertime. It is the little shadow which runs across the grass and loses itself in the sunset."

Was Ispwo Crowfoot a particularly eloquent Indian? Not at all. Fifty-nine years earlier, when George Washington was just a twelve-year-old boy, the Collected Chiefs of the Indian Nations met to discuss a letter from the College of William and Mary suggesting that they "send twelve of their young men to the college, that they might be taught to read and write." The Chiefs sent the following reply:

Sirs,

We know that you highly esteem the kind of learning taught in Colleges, and that the Maintenance of our young Men, while with you, would be very expensive to you. We are convinc'd, therefore, that you mean to do us Good by your Proposal; and we thank you heartily. But you, who are wise, must know that different Nations have different Conceptions of things; and you will therefore not take it amiss, if our Ideas of this kind of Education happen not to be the same with yours. We have some experience of it. Several of our Young People were formerly brought up at the colleges of the Northern Provinces; they were instructed in all your sciences; but, when they came back to us they were bad Runners, ignorant of every means of living in the Woods, unable to bear either Cold or Hunger, knew neither how to build a cabin, take a Deer, or kill an Enemy, spoke our Language imperfectly, were therefore neither fit for Hunters, Warriors, nor Counselors; they were totally good for nothing. We are, however, not the less oblig'd by your kind Offer, tho' we decline accepting it; and, to show our grateful Sense of it, if the Gentlemen of Virginia will send us a Dozen of their Sons, we will take care of their Education; instruct them in all we know, and make Men of them.

Collected Chiefs letter taken from *Letters of a Nation* (edited by Andrew Carroll, published by Broadway Books, 1997)

I wish I could have met the Collected Chiefs who wrote that letter. I wish I could have known Ispwo Crowfoot.

I'm really glad they don't make cowboy and Indian movies anymore. 🙦

96

Sam's Heart and Soul...and Sigh

From the day that Susy was born until her thirteenth birthday, her father, Samuel, wrote innocent and exhilarating adventure stories for children. Toward the end of Sam's life, he wrote, "When Susy was thirteen . . . she secretly, and of her own notion, and out of love, added another task to her labors — the writing of a biography of me."

In this biography of her father, thirteen-year-old Susy tells the world, "We are a very happy family. We consist of Papa, Mamma, Jean, Clara, and me. It is Papa I am writing about, and I shall have no trouble in not knowing what to say about him, as he is a very striking character. He is a very good man and a very funny one — and oh so absent-minded! He does tell perfectly delightful stories. Clara and I used to sit on each arm of his chair and listen while he told us stories about the pictures on the wall."

A well-liberated beagle

A few years later, while Sam was away from home on a trip, Susy died. In a letter to his best friend, Sam wrote, "I did know that Susy was part of us. I did not know that she could go away. I did not know that she could go away and take our lives with her, yet leave our dull bodies behind."

In the years following the death of his daughter, Sam became a devoted atheist and died an angry old man. But we forgive Papa Sam his anger. You and I can easily erase it from memory because, unlike Sam, we never knew his daughter Susy. We remember Sam only for the stories that he told young Susy as she sat on the arm of his chair and stared at the pictures on the wall. We remember Sam, not for Susy Clemens, but for Tom and Huck and Cousin Sid and Becky Thatcher.

And perhaps that's the way it should be. ❧

"Don't part with your illusions. When they are gone you may still exist, but you have ceased to live."

— Mark Twain

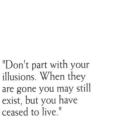

212

97

Dark with Smoldering Eyes

He was a twenty-year-old Scot, she a thirty-six-year-old American with two children. They met when she was traveling alone in Paris; she divorced her husband to marry him.

It was not the Scot's best moment.

Mark Twain described him thusly: "He was most scantily furnished with flesh, his clothes seemed to fall into hollows as if there might be nothing inside but the frame for a sculptor's statue. His long face and lank hair and dark complexion and musing and melancholy expression seemed to fit these details justly and harmoniously, and the altogether of it seemed especially planned to gather the rays of your observation and focalize them upon [his] special distinction and commanding feature, his splendid eyes. They burned with a smoldering rich fire under the penthouse of his brows, and they made him beautiful."

Hoping to win some small measure of acceptance from his new wife's children, the young Scot took them on holiday to his native Scotland. As if in judgment, the weather immediately turned cold and rainy and they were forced to amuse themselves indoors. Seated by the drying fire, the young Scot watched in rapt attention as his twelve-year-old stepson, Lloyd, drew, colored, and annotated the map of an imaginary place. Lloyd's map stimulated our young Scot's imagination, and "on a chill September morning, by the cheek of a brisk fire, I began to write a story based on Lloyd's map as an entertainment for the rest of the family."

Do you remember meeting this "man with the smoldering eyes" so admired by Twain? For it was he that introduced you to young Jim Hawkins, Billy Bones, Captain Flint, and Long John Silver and gave you a place called Treasure Island. We speak his name always in its fullness because he gave us fully of all he had to give: Robert Louis Stevenson.

After giving us his best, he parted, and left us with these few words:

That man is a success who has lived well,
Laughed often and loved much;
Who has gained the respect of intelligent men and the love of
    children;
Who has filled his niche and accomplished his task;
Who leaves the world better than he found it,
Whether by a perfect poem or a rescued soul;
Who never lacked appreciation of the earth's beauty or failed to
    express it;
Who looked for the best in others and gave the best he had.

Are you looking for the best in others? Ralph Waldo Emerson once said, "Every man is entitled to be valued by his best moment."

What will be yours? ৶

SCOTLAND
THE LAND OF ROMANCE

ANCHOR LINE
NEW YORK AND GLASGOW

98

Tom and His Editors

Asking a writer what he thinks about editors is like asking a lamppost what it feels about dogs.

— John Osbourne

Tom is steaming with outrage. He has poured heart and soul into the writing assignment he was given, and now the editing committee is picking his work apart, word by word, phrase by phrase.

Ever been there?

Seeing Tom's frustration, Ben says, "Tom, I once knew a hatmaker who, needing a sign for his shop, drew a little sketch of a hat and wrote above it the words, 'John Thompson, Hatmaker, Fashionable Hats Sold Inside for Ready Money.' As he was taking his sketch to the sign maker, his wife said, 'Who would sell a hat for anything but ready money? Delete that part.' And so he did. Then a friend said, 'And no one cares who made the hats as long as they're good. You should also delete John Thompson, Hatmaker.' And so he did, which left only his picture of a hat with the words, 'Fashionable Hats Sold Inside.' John hadn't gone far before someone looked at the sketch and chuckled 'Who would sell unfashionable hats?' so John removed the word 'Fashionable.' And then another said, 'Who sells hats on the sidewalk? Of course they're sold inside! All you really need is the picture of a hat and above it, the word, 'Hats.'"

"Satisfied that he now had the perfect sign, John showed his sketch to just one more friend. Looking quizzically at it, the friend said, 'You surely don't need the word 'Hats' above the picture, John. All that's needed is the picture itself.' So when he finally arrived at the sign maker's shop, John Thompson had nothing to show him but his little drawing of a hat. Seeing it, the sign maker said, 'Hmmm, this needs something more. Might I suggest that we add your name and occupation, 'John Thompson, Hatmaker,' and perhaps beneath it the words, 'Fashionable Hats Sold Inside for Ready Money?'" Having heard Ben's story, Tom decided not to abandon his writing assignment, and the rest is, quite literally, history.

You will find the original story of the hatmaker's sign in the congressional archives among the papers of Thomas Jefferson, preceded by this notation: "Dr. Franklin perceived that I was not insensitive to Congress' mutilation of my document (the Declaration of Independence) and tried to reassure me by whispering a parable. . . ."

Alas, I fear that H. G. Wells was correct when he said, "No passion in the world is equal to the passion to alter someone else's draft," for if you should locate the original version of Benjamin Franklin's story of the hatmaker's sign and compare it to my account above, you will find that, yes, God forgive me . . . I edited it.

Sorry, Tom. Sorry, Ben.

I'm sorry, Mr. Kipling, but you just don't understand how to use the English language.

> — Publisher's letter to Rudyard Kipling, rejecting his
> *Jungle Book* (1889)

A sheer dead pull from start to finish.

> — Book review of Charles Dickens' *A Tale of Two Cities*
> (1897, *Century Magazine*)

[S]o this is a book of the season only.

> — *New York Herald Tribune* review of F. Scott Fitzgerald's
> *Great Gatsby* (1925)

It is impossible to sell animal stories in the U.S.A.

> — Publisher's rejection letter of George Orwell's
> *Animal Farm* (1945)

The girl doesn't, it seems to me, have a special perception or feeling which would lift that book above the curiosity level.

> — Publisher's rejection letter of Anne Frank's diary (1952)

99

Another Great American
Success Story

aving arrived during the night, we were unprepared for the stunning beauty that awaited us in the morning. Rubbernecking like the tourists we obviously were, Pennie and I were crossing the courtyard of a magnificent Spanish-mission-turned-hotel when we noticed him. We smiled and said, "Buenos dias." He smiled and said hello. We asked if he knew how to get to the hotel restaurant.

His name was Eduardo Prado. Your first impression of Eduardo is that he would make the perfect Latin James Bond. Your second impression is that he beams enough positive energy to be a Spanish Rick Dees. We fell into travelers' conversation. He said he was at the hotel to make arrangements for an upcoming event for FIFA, the world soccer league. We told him that we were in town for a seminar. It was just then that he was joined by his wife, Ana, and the third impression hit both Pennie and me like a tidal wave — JFK and Jackie in the years of Camelot.

Over the next three days we learned that Eduardo and Ana are exactly the same age as Pennie and I and their daughters are the same ages as our sons. We also learned that Eduardo's soccer gig is completely voluntary. Eduardo Prado is the classic self-made millionaire, a two-time pauper and a three-time winner.

Eduardo made his first fortune as a fisherman selling sharkskin to Italian sports car makers. When a huge shipment of sharkskin was hijacked into Mexico, Eduardo was ruined. He even had to pay for the trucks that were stolen. With no money and no prospects, Eduardo lay awake at night asking, "What great need can I fill?" He then made his second fortune by building thousands of small houses for the poor. But since Eduardo wasn't born into a wealthy family, he had no one to turn to when the bank politely informed him one day that he had no money. "What did you do with my seven million?" asked Eduardo. "Exactly which seven million do you mean?" replied the bank. "I'll sue," threatened Eduardo. "How?" smiled the bank. "You have no money."

More sleepless nights as Eduardo planned his third fortune. But this time he vowed to create a business that no one would want to steal. "So I read and studied around the clock to become an expert in sewage disposal." To draw attention to his country's growing sewage problem, Eduardo mocked up a thousand copies of three different ecology magazines, each magazine featuring a story on the country's looming waste-disposal crisis. He mailed the magazines to everyone in government and in the media and followed the mailing with hundreds of telephone calls announcing, "I have a solution."

His third fortune would be his largest by far, and he made it just three years ago.

The story of Eduardo Prado is the Great American Success Story. But in his case it's Central American. You see, my friend Eduardo Prado lives in Guatemala.

For Pennie and me, the next three days would be jammed with a thousand happy surprises, but none quite so jolting as the electric moment that would occur between Eduardo and me exactly one hour after I met him. 🙿

100

A Seat at the Round Table

In the first three minutes that I knew him, Eduardo Prado reminded me of James Bond, of Rick Dees, and of John F. Kennedy. But it was only after seeing Eduardo interact with Guatemala's poorest people that the fourth and final image of him peeked over the horizon of my mind.

This fleeting glimpse happened on the sidewalk outside the hotel where Eduardo and I had met by accident only a few minutes earlier. After pausing to introduce me to a young Guatemalan boy, perhaps fourteen years old and obviously quite poor, Eduardo stared deeply into the young man's eyes, placed his fingers on the boy's cheek, and spoke to him very quietly and fervently in Spanish. When Eduardo was finished, the boy smiled softly and nodded confidently. Eduardo then gently patted the boy's cheek and they parted. In that singularly tender and majestic moment, I was reminded not so much of John F. Kennedy as of England's fabled King Arthur.

"What did you say to him?" I asked. Eduardo said, "I told him that he was an extremely smart young man and that he had a very bright future and that he should never quit believing in it." After a moment of silence, Eduardo continued, "He is a student in a class that I teach." "What kind of class?" I asked. Eduardo looked at me thoughtfully and said, "Are you familiar with the saying, 'Give a man a fish and he eats for a day, teach him to fish and he eats for a lifetime?'" I nodded that I was. Eduardo then smiled a bittersweet smile and said, "I teach the poor how to escape their poverty." Glancing at his watch, he said that he had to leave for an important meeting, but that he and Ana would try to catch up with us later. I walked back into the lobby of the hotel to meet Pennie, Guillermo, Sergio, and

Juan Manuel for a tour of the fabulous 450-year-old mountain city of Antigua, Guatemala.

The first place we went was the Palace. As we turned a corner and stepped into a large room, a crowd of people immediately rose from their seats and turned toward us. Embarrassed, I wondered what we had interrupted. Taking me by the arm, Sergio Garcia led me to the front of the room and motioned that I should sit in an ancient wooden chair. As I did, a pair of elegant gentlemen swept in from doorways on either side of the room to stand at each end of the table opposite me. Then, from behind a curtain at the front of the room, an immaculately dressed gentleman emerged wearing a very large medallion around his neck. Our eyes met in an electric moment of stunned surprise. The man was Eduardo Prado.

Recovering from his shock, Eduardo began speaking to me in Spanish as Sergio Garcia interpreted. "It is good to see you again, my friend. I apologize that now I must speak to you in Spanish only, but the law requires that all official functions be conducted in the Spanish language." After several minutes of regal formalities, Sergio translated, "As Comendador of Antigua, it is my honor to Knight you as Councilor to the Comendador. The appointment is for life. You will henceforth be known as the Don Roy H. Williams." As he placed the large, engraved medallion over my head, Eduardo whispered, "In English, this makes you Sir Roy H. Williams. And by the way, why is there no picture of you in your books? I thought you would be much older."

As we shook hands, I asked Eduardo what the responsibilities of the Comendador's councilor might be. "You are to help me think of ways to help this city and to care for its people. Will you do this?" I replied that I would do so to the best of my ability. I then asked Eduardo whether knighting people was a thing he did often. He replied, "The title you now hold was created by the King of Spain many years ago and was given to a few of the Spanish Conquistadors, but you, my friend, are the first Knight of Antigua in nearly 200 years."

Obviously, Eduardo Prado was hoping that giving me a knighthood would cause the Guatemalan people to become very dear to me and that I would do my best to think of ways to help him help them.

He was right. I will do what I can to help. But my motive isn't tied to any appreciation of the knighthood (although I do enjoy the thought of signing my name "Sir Roy" once in awhile). I plan to help Eduardo Prado because I once saw him lay his hand on the cheek of a poor Guatemalan boy and promise that boy a bright future.

I just want to make sure Eduardo can keep that promise. ❧

100 + 1
Dr. Seuss
on Writing for Children

From *Books of the Century*, by the *New York Times Book Review*, edited by Charles McGrath, copyright © 1998, 2000 by The New York Times Company. Used by permission of Three Rivers Press, a division of Random House, Inc. Originally published in the *New York Times*, November 16, 1952.

There are many reasons why an intelligent man should never ever write for children. Of all professions for a man, it is socially the most awkward. You go to a party, and how do they introduce you? The hostess says, "Dr. Seuss, meet Henry J. Bronkman. Mr. Bronkman manufactures automobiles, jet planes, battleships and bridges. Dr. Seuss . . . well, *he* writes the sweetest, dear, darlingest little whimsies for wee kiddies!"

Mr. Bronkman usually tries to be polite. He admits there *is* a place in the world for such activities. He admits he once was a kiddie himself. He even confesses to having read *Peter Rabbit*. Then abruptly he excuses himself and walks away in search of more vital and rugged companionship.

Wherever a juvenile writer goes, he is constantly subjected to humiliating indignities. When asked to take part in a panel discussion along with other members of the writing fraternity he is given the very end seat at the table . . . always one seat lower than the dusty anthologist who compiled *The Unpublished Letters of Dibble Sneth, Second Assistant Secretary of Something-or-Other under Polk.*

Besides that, since we don't make much money, our friends are always getting us aside and telling us, "Look, now. You can do better. After all, with all your education, there *must* be some way you could crack the Adult Field."

The thing that's so hard to explain to our friends is that most of us who specialize in writing humor for children *have* cracked the adult field and, having cracked it, have decided definitely that we prefer to uncrack it. We are writing for the so-called Brat Field by choice.

222

For, despite the fact this brands us as pariahs, despite the fact this turns us into literary untouchables, there is something we get when we write for the young that we never can hope to get in writing for you ancients. To be sure, in some ways you are superior to the young. You scream less. You burp less. You have fewer public tantrums. You ancients are, generally speaking, slightly more refined. But when it comes to trying to amuse you! . . . Have you ever stopped to consider what has happened to your sense of humor?

When you were a kid named Willy or Mary the one thing you did better than anything else was laugh. The one thing you got more fun out of than anything else was laughing. Why, I don't know. Maybe it has to do with juices. And when somebody knew how to stir those juices for you, you really rolled on the floor. Remember? Your sides almost really did split. Remember? You almost went crazy with the pain of having fun. You were a terrible blitz to your family. So what? Your juices were juicing. Your lava was seething. Your humor was spritzing. You really were living.

At that age you saw life through very clear windows. Small windows, of course. But very bright windows.

And, then, what happened?

You know what happened.

The grown-ups began to equip you with shutters. Your parents, your teachers, your everybody-around-you, your all-of-those-people who loved and adored you . . . they decided your humor was crude and too primitive. You were laughing too loud, too often and too happily. It was time you learned to laugh with a little more restraint.

They began pointing out to you that most of this wonderful giddy nonsense that you laughed at wasn't, after all, quite as funny as you thought.

"Now why," they asked, "are you laughing at *that*? It's completely pointless and utterly ridiculous."

"Nonsense," they told you, "is all right in its place. But it's time you learned how to *keep* it in its place. There's much more in this world than just nonsense."

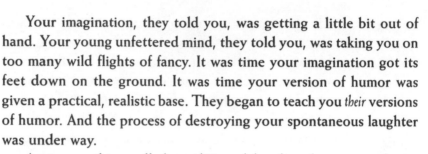

Your imagination, they told you, was getting a little bit out of hand. Your young unfettered mind, they told you, was taking you on too many wild flights of fancy. It was time your imagination got its feet down on the ground. It was time your version of humor was given a practical, realistic base. They began to teach you *their* versions of humor. And the process of destroying your spontaneous laughter was under way.

A strange thing called conditioned laughter began to take its place. Now, conditioned laughter doesn't spring from the juices. It doesn't even spring. Conditioned laughter germinates, like toadstools on a stump.

And, unless you were a very lucky little Willy or Mary, you soon began to laugh at some very odd things. Your laughs, unfortunately, began to get mixed with sneers and smirks.

This conditioned laughter the grown-ups taught you depended entirely on *their* conditions. Financial conditions. Political conditions. Racial, religious and social conditions. You began to laugh at people your family feared or despised — people they felt inferior to, or people they felt better than.

If your father said a man named Herbert Hoover was an ass, and asses should be laughed at, you laughed at Herbert Hoover. Or, if you were born across the street, you laughed at Franklin Roosevelt. Who they were, you didn't know. But the local ground rules said you were to laugh at them. In the same way, you were supposed to guffaw when someone told a story which proved that Swedes are stupid, Scots are tight, Englishmen are stuffy and the Mexicans never wash.

Your laughs were beginning to sound a little tinny. Then you learned it was socially advantageous to laugh at Protestants and/or Catholics. You readily learned, according to your conditions, that you could become the bright boy of the party by harpooning a hook into Jews (or Christians), labor (or capital), or the Turnverein or the Strawberry Festival.

You still laughed for fun, but the fun was getting hemmed in by a world of regulations. You were laughing at subjects according to their listing in the ledger. Every year, as you grew older, the laughs that used to split your sides diminished. The ledger furnished more sophisticated humor. You discovered a new form of humor based on sex. Sex, a taboo subject, called for very specialized laughter. It was a subject that was never considered funny in large gatherings. It was a form of humor you never indulged in at Sunday school. It was a form of humor that was subtle and smart and you learned to restrict it and reserve it for special friends.

And, by the time you had added that accomplishment to your repertoire, you know what had happened to you, Willy or Mary? Your capacity for healthy, silly, friendly laughter was smothered. You'd really grown up. You'd become adults, which is a word that means obsolete children.

As adults, before you laugh, you ask yourselves questions:

"Do I dare laugh at that in the presence of the boss? Sort of dangerous, when you consider how he feels about Taft-Hartley."

"How loud shall I laugh at *that* one? Mrs. Cuthbertson, my hostess, is laughing only fifteen decibels."

"Shall I come right out and say I thought the book was funny? The reviewer in *The Times* said the humor was downright silly."

These are the questions that children never ask. *The Times* reviewer and Mrs. Cuthbertson to the contrary notwithstanding, children never let their laughs out on a string. On their laughter there is no political or social pressure gauge.

That, I think, is why we maverick humorists prefer to write exclusively for children. ❧

I kept this note because it seemed an insightful and fascinating question, artfully written. After teaching the morning session to about 1,200 business owners in the Toronto Convention Center, I found it on the speaker's lectern upon returning from lunch.

Yes, Stephen, even bebafflers can learn to sing.

When bebafflers abound you, can they learn to sing?

Stephen Caissie
Art Director
The Brainstorm Group

WizardSwords

associative memory: a memory that has become linked to another memory.

Augustine's Law: "It is the nature of humans to be attracted by that which is too big to comprehend."

the Beagle: a hungry curiosity, hot on the trail of a discovery.

being Monet: speaking impressionistically, rather than precisely, by using poetic exaggeration and overstatement and selecting words according to the intensity of their associations, or "color." To speak in incomplete sentences due to the removal of "black words." Being Monet might be thought of as radical, accelerated Frosting.

black words: words that do not contribute toward a more vivid and colorful mental image (but, and, that, therefore, etc.)

business problem topology (BPT): the practice of identifying parallel business problems by matching their defining characteristics.

compression: the mind's unconscious tendency to combine or merge gravitating bodies in an effort to reduce complexity.

convergence: a momentary alignment of gravitating bodies in a chaotic system; "the hook."

Crazy Ivan: a non-recurring third gravitating body.

Daguerre: a derogatory term, used to describe a style of writing that is factual, tedious, and colorless. Most academic writing is "Daguerre."

defining characteristics: unusual features or distinguishing elements that are used to identify the "shape" of a business problem.

divergence: the degree of separation between the orbital planes of gravitating bodies in a chaotic system.

first mental image (FMI): the opening scene in a mental sequence.

Frosting: replacing common, predictable phrases with unexpected, interesting ones.

heart of the dog: the internal world of the prospective customer, that realm of hope, fear, prejudice, desire, and ambition.

impact quotient (IQ): an ad's power to convince. IQ can range above and below an average of 1.0.

instantaneity: engaging the imagination with a vivid and electric first mental image (FMI).

last mental image (LMI): the closing scene in a mental sequence.

market potential (MPo): the total dollars available in a business category.

parallel business: in BPT, a business whose solutions to problems are studied in an effort to discover a portable innovation model.

personal experience factor (PEF): an advertiser's reputation, through experience. Like the impact quotient, a PEF score ranges above and below an average of 1.0, with 1.0 being the expectations of the customer. The growth or decline of a company will ultimately follow that company's PEF as it rises and falls above and below 1.0.

putting it under water: editing or deleting information under the assumption that it is already known to the listener.

Robert Frank: a style of writing that is accurate, but very selective in its inclusion of detail, and that approaches the subject from an unusual angle.

Seussing: making up new words that express an idea by virtue of their sound, tone, context, and associations.

share of market: an advertiser's percentage of the total business volume done in his business category.

share of mind: an advertiser's percentage of the customer's total awareness in a product or service category.

share of voice: your company's percentage of all the advertising done in your business category.

surprising Broca: doing or saying the unexpected in an attempt to open the door into the imagination.

Sword in the Stone: the focal idea, the axis around which all else will revolve, the non-negotiable standard at the heart of the company; the North Star in the heart of the client.

Sylvester McMonkey McBean!: "What a great idea! You're going to make a fortune."

third gravitating body: a tiny element that contributes to the creation of a chaotic system; also known as a "horseshoe nail."

transition: a strategic change in third gravitating bodies to reduce the effect of compression.

uncovery: an investigative effort to find an advertiser's unique and wonderful story; "digging for the diamond." Every worthy business has a story that is uniquely and wonderfully its own. The job of the ad writer is to "uncover" this story and tell it.

The Wizard's Index

Psalms, Book of, 122
Putting it under water, 118

Quantum mechanics, 30–31, 34
Questions
  by children, 126–127
  for children, 154–155
  examples of daily questions of author, 156–157
  wording of, 101

Radio
  advertising on, 79, 82, 85, 116
  business problem topology for radio stations, 72–73
  primetime for, 96
  time spent listening (TSL) study on, 85
Radio stations, 72–73
Rainbows, 186–187
Rand, Ayn, 31
Random House, 55–56
Random systems, 119
"Ravenna" (Wilde), 176
Reach-and-frequency analysis, 96
Reach of advertising, 82–83
Reagan, Ronald, 179
Reality. *See also* Perceptual realities
  four-dimensional reality, 16–17, 32, 34, 42, 132, 135
  objective reality, 18–19
  one-dimensional reality, 34–35, 42
  three-dimensional reality, 16–17, 32–33, 34, 42, 132, 135
  two-dimensional reality, 32–33, 34, 42
Reason versus emotion, 28–29. *See also* Thought
Reductionism, 26–27
Reformation. *See* Protestant Reformation
Relativity of Wrong (Asimov), 100–101
Relativity theory, 30–31, 34, 42, 92
Relevance. *See* Impact quotient (IQ)
Religion. *See also* Bible
  authority of, 29
  Protestant Reformation, 200
Renoir, Auguste, 48
Republic National Bank of New York, 191
Research steps, 156
Responsibility, 182–183
Rest, 136–137, 140–147
Revolutionary War, 178
Ries, Al, 114
Ries, Laura, 114
Right and wrong, 100–101
Right brain. *See also* Left brain
  as abstract thought, 36–39
  anapests and, 111–112
  attention and, 64
  "auditory" people and, 57
  decision making and, 64
  "down" metaphor for, 23
  educational system and, 60–61
  emotions and, 20–23, 64
  energy and, 64
  first- and third-dimensional reality and, 42
  functions of, 20–23

humor and, 112
introversion and, 64
intuition and, 64, 126–127
mental movie screen of, 26–27
mental participation and, 112
need for both left brain and, 62
and one as number of unity, 34
organization skills and, 65
perceiving and, 65
poetry and, 21
preference profiling and, 63–66
songs and, 20–21
subliminal associations and, 112–113
symbolic thought and, 36–37, 69–70
techniques for access to, 111–113
tension between left brain and, 28–29
Risk taking, 138–139
Robards, Lewis, 179
Robards, Rachel Donelson, 178–179
Robbins, Steve, 91
Robbins, Tom, 17, 62, 73, 132, 189
Robblee, Steve, 103
Robert Frank writing style, 117–118
Robinson, Ken, 60
Rockne, Knute, 154
"Romantic" languages, 23
Romanticism and science, 62
Rome, 194
Roper Starch Worldwide, 134
Rosenthal, Joe, 192–193
Rostler, William, 149
Rothschild, Baron Nathan Mayer de, 190–191
Rules, 32–33, 34, 42, 114–115
Ryan, Ed, 160
Ryan, Meg, 27

Sales. *See* Selling
Sales resistance, 80
Sales training, 80
Saliency. *See* Impact quotient (IQ)
Santayana, George, 137
Saturday Night Live, 208
Saxe, John Godfrey, 14
Schools. *See* Education
Schwarzkopf, H. Norman, 178
Science. *See also* Neurology; Physics
  authority of, 29
  English language and, 22–23
  left brain and scientific outlook, 22–23, 26–27
  and romanticism, 62
  symbolic thought and, 37
Scotland, 213
Security and opportunity, 68, 69–71
Sejnowski, Terence, 82
Self-knowledge, preference profiling for, 63–66
Seligman, Martin, 150
Selling
  ad writers and, 85
  in jewelry stores, 90–91
  relationship of salespersons and customers, 80

About the Wizard

Nicknamed "the Wizard of Ads" by an early client, Roy H. Williams, along with his talented and creative staff, has been the unseen, pivotal force in some amazing, come-from-behind victories in the worlds of politics, business, and finance. "David faced Goliath with nothing but his faith and five smooth stones," says Williams. "We like to think of ourselves as being among those stones."

Once a month, Williams teaches creative thinking, strategic planning, and human persuasion in a three-day Wizard Academy that is attended by advertising agencies, college professors, CEOs, small-business owners, broadcasters, and journalists from around the world.* His books consistently attain bestseller status and have been translated for international distribution in China, Brazil, Korea, and Israel.

A lifelong student of the human race, Williams is forever seeking to answer the question, "What makes people do the things they do?" The answers that he discovers along the way provide a wealth of practical knowledge as well as a constant source of entertainment to his students and friends around the world.

The Wizard lives in the middle of nowhere, Texas, with Pennie, "The Princess of the World."

* When they arrive, they're seated next to fellow students from many of the world's largest and most successful advertising agencies (J. Walter Thompson, Young & Rubicam) and executives from some of the world's largest corporations (biggest so far: Procter and Gamble). To apply for admission into the growing fraternity of Wizard Academy graduates, just call **512-295-5700** or visit **www.wizardacademy.com**. The curriculum is highly interactive, so class size is usually held to about a dozen students.

Roy H. Williams
Williams Marketing, Inc.
1760 FM 967
Buda, TX 78610

(Is this an ad for Wizard Academy? Yes. But hey, I'm an advertising guy, remember?)

238

(1470) ENGRAVING and PRINTING

(80)

(90) Discovery of AMERICA

" " way to INDIA

(1500)

(10) Albuquerque in India

(20) MAGELLAN'S voyage
GEMMA FRISIUS, terr...
(30) J Ferrel: Length of ord...

(40) Cartier on St Lawrence

Copernicus, solar syste...

(1550)

(60)

(70) Digges, theodolite 157...
DRAKE'S voyages

(80)

(90) Plane table

(1600)

(10) Hudson's voyages
Champlain's voyages
Snellius TRIANGUL...

(20)

(30)

(40) Tasman's voyage
Barometer (Torricelli)
Cossacks reach ...

(1650)

Pendulum clock

(60)

(70) PICARD { length of arc, longitudes, use of telescope }
Joliet & Marquette, Missi...sippi R.

(80) Newton, ⊖ spheroid

(90)

(1700)

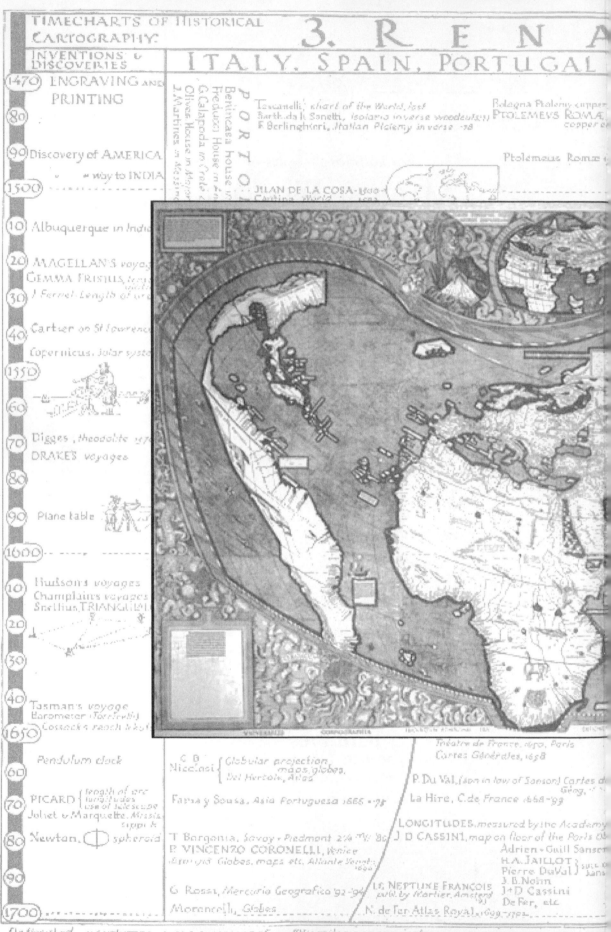

PORTO...

Toscanelli, chart of the World, lost
Barth. da li Sonetti, Isolario in verse woodcuts(?)
F. Berlinghieri, Italian Ptolemy in verse -78

Benincasa house in ...
Freducci House in ...
G. Calapoda in Crete ...
Olives House in Messin...
J. Martines in Messina

Bologna Ptolemy copper...
PTOLEMEVS ROMÆ
copper en...

Ptolemaus Romæ ...

JUAN DE LA COSA -1500-
Cantino World ...1502

C. B. Nicolosi { Globular projection, maps, globes. Dal Hercole, Atlas

Faria y Sousa, Asia Portuguesa 1666 - 75

T. Borgonio, Savoy - Piedmont 2¼ M/" 80
P. VINCENZO CORONELLI, Venice
... Globes, maps etc. Atlante Veneto 1690

G. Rossi, Mercurio Geografico '92 -'94

Morencelli, Globes

Théatre de France, 1650, Paris
Cartes Générales, 1658

P. Du Val, (son in law of Sanson) Cartes de... Géog.

La Hire, C. de France 1668-99

LONGITUDES, measured by the Academy
J D CASSINI, map on floor of the Paris Ob...
Adrien - Guill Sanson
H.A. JAILLOT }
Pierre DuVal }
J. B. Nolin
J + D Cassini
De Fer, etc.

LE NEPTUNE FRANÇOIS
publ. by Hubier, Amsterd...

N. de Fer Atlas Royal, 1699-1702.